Contents

KU-481-911

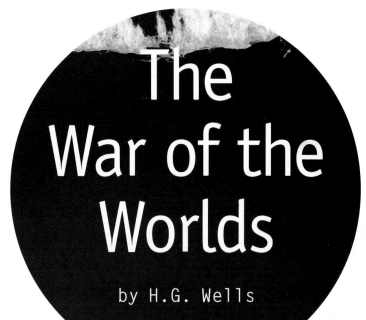

The War of the Worlds

by H.G. Wells

...ter Morrisson

...ies Editors:
...e Bennett and Dave Stockwin

The Publishers would like to thank the following for permission to reproduce copyright material.

Photo credits

p. 9 Ingram; **p. 11** NASA/JPL-Caltech; **p. 17** Ingram; **p. 32** Moviestore Collection Ltd/Alamy; **p. 43** Paramount Pictures/TopFoto; **p. 48** TopFoto; **p. 53** The Art Archive/Alamy; **p. 55** Ingram

Acknowledgements

Extracts from *The War of the Worlds* © United Agents. Permission applied for.

Every effort has been made to trace all copyright holders, but if any have been inadvertently overlooked, the Publishers will be pleased to make the necessary arrangements at the first opportunity.

Although every effort has been made to ensure that website addresses are correct at time of going to press, Hodder Education cannot be held responsible for the content of any website mentioned in this book. It is sometimes possible to find a relocated web page by typing in the address of the home page for a website in the URL window of your browser.

Hachette UK's policy is to use papers that are natural, renewable and recyclable products and made from wood grown in sustainable forests. The logging and manufacturing processes are expected to conform to the environmental regulations of the country of origin.

Orders: please contact Bookpoint Ltd, 130 Park Drive, Milton Park, Abingdon, Oxon OX14 4SE. Telephone: (44) 01235 827720. Fax: (44) 01235 400454. Email education@bookpoint.co.uk Lines are open from 9 a.m. to 5 p.m., Monday to Saturday, with a 24-hour message answering service. You can also order through our website: www.hoddereducation.co.uk

ISBN: 978 1 4718 5370 8

© Peter Morrisson, 2016

First published in 2016 by

Hodder Education,

An Hachette UK Company

Carmelite House

50 Victoria Embankment

London EC4Y 0DZ

www.hoddereducation.co.uk

Impression number   10 9 8 7 6 5 4 3 2

Year   2020 2019 2018 2017

Cover photo © Vadim Sadovski/123RF.com

Typeset in 11/13pt Bliss Light by Integra Software Services Pvt. Ltd., Pondicherry, India

Printed in Dubai

A catalogue record for this title is available from the British Library.

Getting the most from this guide

This guide is designed to help you to raise your achievement in your examination response to *The War of the Worlds*. It is intended for you to use throughout your GCSE English literature course. It will help you when you are studying the novel for the first time and also during your revision.

The following features have been used throughout this guide to help you focus your understanding of the novel.

Target your thinking

A list of **introductory questions** labelled by Assessment Objective is provided at the beginning of each chapter to give you a breakdown of the material covered. They target your thinking, in order to help you work more efficiently by focusing on the key messages.

Build critical skills

These boxes offer an opportunity to consider some **more challenging questions**. They are designed to encourage deeper thinking, analysis and exploratory thought. Building and practising critical skills in this way will give you a real advantage in the examination.

GRADE *FOCUS*

It is possible to know a novel well and yet still underachieve in the examination if you are unsure what the examiners are looking for. The **GRADE FOCUS** boxes give a clear explanation of **how you may be assessed**, with an emphasis on the criteria for gaining a Grade 5 and a Grade 8.

REVIEW YOUR LEARNING

At the end of each chapter you will find this section to **test your knowledge**: a series of short, specific questions to ensure that you have understood and absorbed the key messages of the chapter. Answers to the 'Review your learning' questions are provided in the final section of the guide (p. 101).

GRADE *BOOSTER*

Read and remember these pieces of helpful **grade-boosting advice**. They provide top tips from experienced teachers and examiners who can advise you on what to do, as well as what *not* to do, in order to maximise your chances of success in the examination.

Key quotation

Key quotations are highlighted for you, so that if you wish you may use them as **supporting evidence** in your examination answers. Further quotations, grouped by characterisation, theme and key moments, can be found in the 'Top ten quotations' section on page 94 of the guide. All page references in this guide refer to the 2005 edition of *The War of the Worlds*, published by Penguin Classics (ISBN 9780141441030).

'What are these Martians?'

'What are we?' I answered, clearing my throat.
(Book 1, Ch. 13, p. 70)

Studying the text

You may find it useful to read sections of this guide when you need them, rather than reading it from start to finish. For example, the 'Context' section can be read before you read the novel itself, since it offers an explanation of the relevant historical, cultural and literary background to the text. It is here that you will find information about aspects of Wells's life and times which influenced his writing, the particular issues with which Wells was concerned and where the novel stands in terms of the literary tradition to which it belongs.

As you work through the novel, you may find it helpful to read the relevant 'Plot and structure' sections before or after reading a particular chapter. As well as a summary of events there is also commentary, so that you are aware both of key events and features in each of the chapters. The sections on 'Characterisation', 'Themes' and 'Language, style and analysis' will help to develop your thinking further, in preparation for written responses on particular aspects of the text.

Many students also enjoy the experience of being able to bring something extra to their classroom lessons in order to be 'a step ahead of the game'. Alternatively, you may have missed a classroom session or feel that you need a clearer explanation and the guide can help you with this too.

An initial reading of the section on 'Assessment Objectives and skills' will enable you to make really effective notes in preparation for assessments. The Assessment Objectives are what examination boards base their mark schemes on. In this section they are broken down and clearly explained.

Revising the text

Whether you study the novel in a block of time close to the exam or much earlier in your GCSE literature course, you will need to revise thoroughly if you are to achieve the very best grade that you can.

You should first remind yourself of what happens in the novel and so the chapter on 'Plot and structure' might be returned to in the first instance. You might then look at the 'Assessment Objectives and skills' section to ensure that you understand what the examiners are looking for in general, and then look carefully at the 'Tackling the exams' section.

'Tackling the exams' gives you useful information on question format, depending on which examination board specification you are following, as well as practical advice on the examination format, and practical considerations such as the time available for the question and the Assessment Objectives which apply to it. Advice is also supplied on how to approach the question, writing a quick plan, and 'working with' the text, since all of the examination boards use an extract-based question for *The War of the Worlds*. Focused advice on how you might improve your grade follows, and you need to read this section carefully.

You will also find examples of exam-style responses in the 'Sample essays' section, with examiner's comments in the margins, so that you can see clearly how to move towards a Grade 5 and how to then move from Grade 5 to Grade 8.

Now that all GCSE literature examinations are 'closed book', the 'Top ten quotations' section will be an invaluable aid, in that it offers you the opportunity to learn short quotations to support points about character and themes as well as a revision aid which identifies the top ten key moments in the novel.

When writing about the novel, use this guide as a springboard to develop your own ideas. Remember that the examiners are not looking for set responses. You should not read this guide in order to memorise chunks of it, ready to regurgitate in the exam. Identical answers are dull. The examiners hope to reward you for perceptive thought, individual appreciation and varying interpretations. They want to sense that you have engaged with the themes and ideas in the novel, explored Wells's methods with an awareness of the context in which he wrote, and enjoyed this part of your literature course.

There are, of course, a number of film versions of *The War of the Worlds*, ranging from the 1953 classic starring Gene Barry to the 2005 Steven Spielberg blockbuster starring Tom Cruise. However, you will find interesting differences to the text in all of them. For example, in the Spielberg version, the narrator has a name, is divorced and is a macho crane operator working on a New Jersey dock as opposed to being a happily married member of the English middle-class intelligentsia! All of these are enjoyable versions of the tale which convey the essential message of the novel. However, they should never be seen as a substitute for the text itself. For instance, examiners are unlikely to be impressed by responses which refer to the narrator as 'Ray'!

Enjoy referring to the guide as you study the text, and good luck in your exam.

Context

Target your thinking

- What is 'context'? (**AO3**)
- How did H. G. Wells's life influence his writing? (**AO3**)
- To what extent are historical events an influence on *The War of the Worlds*? (**AO3**)
- Which literary and cultural influences inspired the writing of the novel? (**AO3**)
- Is the novel still relevant to modern readers? (**AO3**)

What is 'context'?

The 'context' of a novel means the circumstances in which it was written — the social, historical, intellectual and literary factors that influenced what the author wrote. All literature is influenced by the life experiences of the author and these are shaped by the world in which he or she lived. Therefore, in order to truly understand *The War of the Worlds* (1897–1898), it is necessary to have some understanding of both Wells's life and his world.

Biographical context

H. G. Wells's early years

Herbert George Wells was born on 21 September 1866, in Bromley, Kent, which was a small market town on the outskirts of London. When he was aged thirteen, his family broke up as a result of financial hardship and the young Wells was forced to give up school and seek work. In 1881, he was apprenticed to a department store in Southsea, Portsmouth, which he found a miserable experience. In 1883, Wells managed to cancel his apprenticeship and in September 1884 he began a degree course at the Normal School of Science, South Kensington in London thanks to a government scholarship.

Education

Wells was fortunate enough to be taught biology and zoology by one of the leading thinkers of the day, Darwin's friend and devotee, T. H. Huxley. Although inspired by Huxley's teaching, Wells became tired of the course and left the college in 1887 without a degree. The influence of Darwinism on Wells's novel, *The War of the Worlds*, will be discussed later in this chapter.

By the summer of 1887, Wells was a science teacher in a small private school in North Wales. Unfortunately, he became ill as result of being severely underfed while he was a student and, after being injured on the football pitch, he suffered serious kidney and lung damage. It is no wonder that the struggle to eke out food features as such an important theme in *The War of the Worlds*.

In 1890, Wells finally fulfilled his academic potential by gaining a first-class degree in zoology from the University of London. He then began work as a tutor in biology for the University Correspondence College.

During his time as a tutor, Wells also began to develop a career as a writer and a journalist. His first book, published in 1893, was a science textbook entitled *Textbook of Biology*.

Build critical skills

Re-read *The War of the Worlds*, Book 2, Chapter 2, and then consider how Wells uses his deep interest in and understanding of biology when creating his Martians' unusual digestive processes.

Early writings

Shortly after the publication of this work, Wells again suffered ill health and had to resign his teaching post and live entirely off his writing. Fortunately, he was able to make a successful living writing short stories and essays for the press which existed at the time.

In 1895, Wells published his first novel, *The Time Machine,* and this sci-fi adventure about a philosophical time traveller became an immediate success. This resulted in a quick succession of novels which included:

- *The Island of Dr Moreau* (1896)
- *The Invisible Man* (1897)
- *The War of the Worlds* (1898)
- *When the Sleeper Awakes* (1899)
- *The First Men in the Moon* (1901)

By 1901, Wells had established himself as a popular and prolific author in both England and America and his books were rapidly being translated into a variety of languages. By the time of his death in 1946, Wells had published more than fifty works of fiction (not all of them science fiction) as well as a great many non-fiction books and pamphlets.

Later work

During the twentieth century, Wells became more politically active. In the early 1920s he became a prospective Labour MP, indicating the strength of his convictions about the importance of a fairer society. However, his ideas were much bigger than even this. In *The Open Conspiracy*, published in 1928, Wells

▲ H. G. Wells

promotes the idea of global government and global citizenship as an alternative to the nationalism which had helped create the First World War, and which would ultimately result in the Second World War.

Patrick Parrinder, author of the biographical note in the Penguin Classics edition of *The War of the Worlds*, states 'The proposal set out in his Penguin Special *The Rights of Man* (1940) helped to bring about the United Nations declaration of 1948', in which case, it might be the most influential thing that Wells ever wrote!

Wells died in London on 13 August 1946, at a time when Great Britain and much of the rest of the world was busily engaged on the gargantuan task of reconstruction in the aftermath of the Second World War.

Social, historical and intellectual context

Earlier novels about Martians

When writing *The War of the Worlds,* Wells was certainly not writing in a vacuum. Authors never are! In 1880, Percy Greg had published a novel entitled *Across the Zodiac* in which a traveller journeys to Mars and discovers an advanced civilisation rather similar to that of the Earth. The Martians are humanoid (man-like), though not as tall as we are, which certainly rings a bell with some of today's supposedly true-life alien abduction accounts.

In 1897, the same year in which Wells began writing *The War of the Worlds*, German author Kurd Lasswitz published *On Two Planets*. A group of Arctic explorers discover a Martian base at the North Pole. The humanoid Martians transport some of the explorers back to Mars where they discover a highly advanced civilisation with a most sophisticated canal system. Interestingly, the novel also includes a battle in which the Martians pulverise the Royal Navy. As Lasswitz was German, and as there was a great rivalry between the two countries, this explains the prejudice being expressed here.

Although Lasswitz's novel was not translated into English until 1971, it does rather appear as if Wells is directly responding to this slur on British naval prowess when in *The War of the Worlds* he has the Royal Navy warship, *Thunder Child*, give the Martians an undoubted 'black eye' as it destroys at least two Martian tripods. For all Wells's visionary thinking and his critiquing of British society, his patriotism and pride in the British armed forces is demonstrated here, and on a number of occasions elsewhere in the novel.

Of course, one distinction between Wells's depiction of the Martians and that of these other two novels is that Wells's Martians are definitely not humanoid.

Life on Mars?

Wells's vision of the planet Mars itself owes much to the astronomer Percival Lowell's supposedly scientific book, *Mars,* published in 1895. Based solely on very imperfect observations from his newly constructed observatory in Flagstaff, Arizona, USA, Lowell's pseudo-scientific text conjures up highly poetic images of a dying planet upon which an advanced civilisation has constructed a series of irrigation canals in order to carry water from the Martian polar caps in a desperate effort to sustain itself.

According to the *Oxford English Dictionary*, pseudo-science (as written by Lowell) is 'a collection of beliefs or practices mistakenly regarded as being based on scientific method'. By contrast, in *The War of the Worlds*, Wells is writing **quasi-science**.

quasi-science: pretend science

GRADE *BOOSTER*

```
Showing an awareness in your responses that Wells
deliberately uses scientific references and
terminology (quasi-science) to create the illusion
that he is writing science when, in fact, he
is writing fiction will reveal your detailed
understanding of his use of language.
```

The 'canals' that Lowell had been observing were actually optical illusions created by natural surface features on Mars distantly observed through the insufficiently powerful telescopes of the day.

Despite the preposterous nature of his fanciful ideas about there being an advanced civilisation on Mars, Lowell was an extremely able astronomer

▲ NASA science rover approaching Mars, depicted by an artist

and proposed the existence of Pluto which was eventually discovered in 1930 about 6 degrees from his predicted position.

Darwinian evolution

Possibly the most important scientific publication of the nineteenth century was Charles Darwin's *On the Origin of Species* (1859). Darwin argues for a model of the world in which organisms evolve into ever more complex organisms over an immense period of time. In the chapter entitled *Struggle for Existence*, Darwin declares:

> The action of climate seems at first sight to be quite independent of the struggle for existence; but in so far as climate chiefly acts in reducing food, it brings on the most severe struggle between the individuals, whether of the same or of distinct species, which subsist on the same kind of food.

Such ideas as this have clearly shaped Wells's writing of *The War of the Worlds*. Regarding the main action of the Martian invasion, Wells has the narrator state 'That last stage of exhaustion, which to us is still incredibly remote, has become a present-day problem for the inhabitants of Mars' (Book 1, Ch. 1, p. 8). Mars is clearly a dying planet and thus through 'the immediate pressure of necessity', which has further enhanced their evolution in that it 'has brightened their intellects' (p. 8), the Martians launch their invasion upon the vibrant planet Earth in an effort to survive.

Key quotation

And looking across space with instruments and intelligences such as we have scarcely dreamed of, they see, at its nearest distance only 35,000,000 of miles sunward of them, a morning star of hope, our own warmer planet, green with vegetation and grey with water, with a cloudy atmosphere eloquent of fertility...
(Book 1, Ch. 1, p. 8)

In fact, so gruesome and powerful is the theme of food within the novel that rather than just steal our food, the Martians actually feed directly on us!

Key quotation

Their undeniable preference for men as their source of nourishment is partly explained by the nature of the remains of the victims they had brought with them as provisions from Mars.
(Book 2, Ch. 2, p. 126)

Key quotation

Then he would suddenly revert to the matter of the food I withheld from him, praying, begging, weeping, at last threatening.
(Book 2, Ch. 4, p. 137)

More subtly, Darwin's dark vision of a universe in which individuals and species struggle violently over limited resources, particularly food, is also played out in the subplot between the curate and the narrator in the house in Sheen.

Darwin and Christianity

Darwin's theory of living creatures evolving into ever more complex forms over millions of years created immense philosophical, intellectual and emotional turmoil at the time of its publication in 1859 because it challenged the fundamental Christian belief that God had created all things in just six days. Darwin's ideas also suggest that the world is many times older than the Bible indicates. It raised the question that if the Bible could not be trusted on this crucial point concerning the creation of life, what other errors might it contain?

A further impact of Darwin's findings was to suggest a world in which the predominant principle is 'the survival of the fittest'. This is a vision of an uncaring universe in which the weak are destroyed by the strong and in which God does not intervene. A number of these ideas had already surfaced prior to Darwin's publication. They had obviously influenced the famous poet Alfred Tennyson when he wrote of 'Nature, red in tooth and claw' in his epic poem *In Memoriam* (published in 1850).

Sir Charles Lyell's *Principles of Geology*, published in 1830–33, had argued there was no evidence to support the biblical account of Noah's Flood and that the world was significantly older than the 6,000 years or so which some theologians believed it to be. The current scientific estimate of the age of the earth is 4.54 billion years!

GRADE **BOOSTER**

```
Insights into the cultural background of the novel,
such as the move towards secularisation in Victorian
times, may gain you credit in the exam if used
relevantly and to demonstrate an enhanced understanding
of the novel.
```

secularisation: when a society places less importance on religious beliefs and values

The blending of Christian ideas and evolutionary theory

Although the theory of evolution presents a severe challenge to the biblical account of creation as described in Genesis, the first book in the Old Testament, it is not necessarily an outright challenge to the belief in God. In fact, Darwin did not actually deny the existence of God, although he did think of himself as an **agnostic**.

In the world of the novel, Wells incorporates both the theory of Darwinian evolution and the idea of an ultimately benevolent God. The Martians are superior to the human race because their planet is much older

agnostic: a person that neither believes nor disbelieves in God due to the lack of absolutely conclusive evidence either way

Key quotation

The physiological advantages of the practice of injection are undeniable, if one thinks of the tremendous waste of human time and energy occasioned by eating and the digestive process.
(Book 2, Ch. 2, p. 125)

Key quotation

...slain, after all man's devices had failed, by the humblest things that God, in his wisdom, has put upon this earth.
(Book 2, Ch. 8, p. 168)

Key quotation

Yet so vain is man, and so blinded by his vanity...
(Book 1, Ch. 1, p. 8)

and so they have been evolving for much longer. In Book 2, Chapter 2, Wells uses his understanding of biology to paint a lurid picture of the Martian digestive process, which the narrator regards as being far more evolutionarily advanced than that of humans.

Fortunately, the human race is eventually safeguarded through naturally occurring bacteria which kill the Martians.

However, Wells's presentation of the role of God within the novel is also as a supreme being who wants to teach the human race a serious lesson:

> For a moment I believed that the destruction of Sennacherib had been repeated, that God had repented, that the Angel of Death had slain them in the night.

(Book 2, Ch. 8, p. 169)

The biblical reference seems to suggest that God has relented and decided to spare humanity from total destruction. As Wells makes clear in the opening chapter, 'man' is arrogant and vicious, the main example given being the behaviour of British colonists in Tasmania earlier in the century. In fact, it may well be the case that when Wells refers to 'man' in this opening chapter, he is more specifically referring to the British Empire.

Therefore, the punishment of man via the Martian invasion is justified. And as a result of the human race being spared, the final chapter of the novel informs us that a better human race has arisen.

Key quotation

It may be that in the larger design of the universe this invasion from Mars is not without its ultimate benefit for men; it has robbed us of that serene confidence in the future which is the most fruitful source of decadence...and it has done much to promote the conception of the commonweal of mankind.
(Book 2, Ch. 10, p. 179)

Thomas Carlyle and the politics of the Apocalypse

The Apocalypse is defined by the *Oxford English Dictionary* as 'the complete final destruction of the world, as described in the biblical book of Revelation'. The Book of Revelation comes at the end of the New Testament, the second part of the Bible.

This powerful theological theme, which runs throughout English literature, featured prominently in the work of Thomas Carlyle. Carlyle (1795–1881) was a Scottish philosopher, essayist and historian who was regarded as one of the most important social commentators of his time. The great Victorian novelist, Charles Dickens, dedicated his novel, *Hard Times,* to him in 1854.

Carlyle often used apocalyptic imagery. For example, in the highly **satirical**, yet deadly serious, *Sartor Resartus* (1833–34), Carlyle gives the following words to his fictional editor:

> that the monster UTILITARIA, held back, indeed, and moderated by nose-rings, halters, foot-shackles, and every conceivable modification of rope, should go forth to do her work;—to tread down old ruinous Palaces and Temples with her broad hoof, till the whole were trodden down, that new and better might be built!

satirical: satirical writing uses humour to make a moral point by making fun of the vice or folly of someone or something

Carlyle is referring to utilitarianism, which was a nineteenth-century doctrine which suggested that the rightness of an action should be determined by the extent to which it promoted the general good of society. However, critics such as Carlyle regarded it as dangerous because it sought to replace religion with reason and logic. Here utilitarianism is portrayed as a demonic monster which has come to end the world.

In many respects, the style of writing which Wells creates for the unnamed narrator in *The War of the Worlds* resembles Carlyle's style of mixing history and social criticism.

Millenarianism

The idea of the Apocalypse is often associated with millenarianism — the belief in a thousand-year period of blessedness on Earth. Unfortunately, this period of grace arises out of the global destruction brought about by the Apocalypse. As the nineteenth century was drawing to a close, and the new millennium in the form of the twentieth century was about to dawn, it was a most appropriate time for Wells to tap into such *fin de siècle* anxiety when plotting out his sci-fi horror masterpiece.

International relations

The War of the Worlds is also very firmly rooted in the international politics of the day. After the accession to power of the young Kaiser Wilhelm II in 1888, Germany adopted a more aggressive and expansionist foreign policy, which was bent on building an empire which could rival that of Great Britain. In a Reichstag debate in December 1897, German Foreign Secretary Bernhard von Bülow declared: '...we demand our own place in the sun.'

Concerns about a German invasion were expressed as far back as 1871 by a British army officer by the name of George Chesney who wrote a novel entitled *The Battle of Dorking* in which an unprepared Britain is successfully invaded by a superior foreign force, which employs a new invention described as 'fatal engines' in order to destroy the Royal Navy.

Key quotation

I was...busy upon a series of papers discussing the probable developments of moral ideas as civilization progressed.
(Book 1, Ch. 1, p. 12)

fin de siècle: literally means end of the century but, in terms of the late nineteenth century, it also encompasses the notion of a whole era coming to an end

The Battle of Dorking is regarded as an influential novel in that it helped create a market for what has become known as 'invasion literature'. In what ways might it have been an influence on Wells's writing of *The War of the Worlds*?

In order to support such ambitions, between 1906 and 1914 Germany engaged with Britain in what has become known as the naval race as Britain tried to counter Germany's attempt to build a navy large and powerful enough to rival the global reach of the British Navy. This clearly led to rising tensions between the two countries. Wells alludes to this rivalry in *The War of the Worlds* when he has his narrator comment:

> Many people had heard of the cylinder, of course, and talked about it in their leisure, but it certainly did not make the sensation that an ultimatum to Germany would have done.
>
> (Book 1, Ch. 8, p. 35)

In many respects, *The War of the Worlds* can be read as raising an amazingly prophetic concern about the potential transformation of warfare into something vastly more mechanised and deadly which, of course, is what the First World War became. Speaking in 1920, Wells said:

> A few of us were trying to point out the obvious possibilities of flying, of great guns, of poison gas, and so forth in presently making life uncomfortable if some sort of world peace was not assured, but the books we wrote were regarded as the silliest of imaginative gymnastics. Well, the world knows better now.

Empire

The novel is also a reflection of Wells's concerns about the moral condition of the British Empire. The years 1815–1914 have been described as 'Britain's imperial century'. By the early twentieth century, the British Empire encompassed around twenty per cent of the Earth's surface and incorporated around twenty-five per cent of the world's population. In *The War of the Worlds,* it is obvious that Wells's narrator undoubtedly admires the fire power and courage of the British armed forces. For example, the heroics of the *Thunder Child* are enthusiastically described in Book 1, Chapter 17; and in Book 2, Chapter 9, the narrator pointedly mentions the Union Jack flying above the sixth cylinder. However, the Martians' brutal colonisation of southeast England is a deliberate parallel of how the British Empire used its industrial and technological superiority to subdue and then exploit its subject peoples across the world, for example in New Zealand and Tasmania.

GRADE BOOSTER

Asymmetric warfare occurs when one side is significantly more militarily powerful than the other side. The examiner will be impressed if you are able to make a relevant parallel between the asymmetric warfare waged by the Martians against humanity and the asymmetric warfare waged by the British Empire against less technologically advanced societies.

Key quotation

And before we judge of them too harshly we must remember what ruthless and utter destruction our own species has wrought, not only upon animals, such as the vanished bison and the dodo, but upon its own inferior races. The Tasmanians, in spite of their human likeness, were entirely swept out of existence in a war of extermination waged by European immigrants, in the space of fifty years.
(Book 1, Ch. 1, p. 9)

Furthermore, 1897, the year in which the novel was serialised, was a Jubilee year and Queen Victoria's sixty years on the British throne was being widely celebrated. On the opening page of the novel, Wells has his narrator comment:

> With infinite complacency men went to and fro over this globe about their little affairs, serene in their assurance of their empire over matter.

(p. 7)

This is almost certainly a direct reference to the British Empire — in fact, the word 'empire' is explicitly mentioned — and it might have been that one of Wells's intentions in writing the novel was to counteract this spirit of national self-congratulation which was very much to the fore at the time.

Key quotation

It may be that in the larger design of the universe this invasion from Mars is not without its ultimate benefit for men; it has robbed us of that serene confidence in the future which is the most fruitful source of decadence…
(Book 2, Ch. 10, p. 179)

Industrialisation

A further factor which might well have shaped the novel is the ongoing industrial revolution. The massive growth of heavily polluted industrial towns which were expanding ever more into the surrounding English countryside was a factor which threatened to destabilise the entire fabric of Victorian England. It created great wealth for a new entrepreneurial minority who were astute enough to set up factories and mills or who created other related businesses that advanced Britain's trade and commerce. However, it also led to the ruthless exploitation of the largely unskilled and uneducated workers who were needed as manual labour to keep the machines running.

It is interesting how Wells presents the Martians as mechanical geniuses who employ fire, smoke and machinery in order to terrorise and destroy acres of the peaceful rural landscape, and their local populations, as they press onwards towards London. In this respect, they could be read as a metaphor for the physically destructive force of industrialisation.

▲ Queen Victoria

Key quotation

Key quotation

Outside there began a metallic hammering, then a violent hooting, and then again, after a quiet interval, a hissing like the hissing of an engine.
(Book 2, Ch. 1, p. 121)

Build critical skills

The late-eighteenth-century invention of machinery that could replace the work of humans in manufacturing has ultimately led to man leaving behind the horse and cart and establishing a permanent presence in space. In what other ways do you think that the industrial revolution has transformed the way in which we live?

However, the symbolic significance of the Martian invasion might also be viewed at an even deeper level. Thomas Carlyle, in his 1829 essay, *A Mechanical Age*, had written passionately about the psychological harm being done to the human race as a result of this new and world-changing industrial revolution:

> Not the external and physical alone is now managed by machinery, but the internal and spiritual also…The same habit regulates not our modes of action alone, but our modes of thought and feeling. Men are grown mechanical in head and heart, as well as in hand.'

metaphor: when something is said to be something that it literally is not

Carlyle is intentionally using machinery as a **metaphor** to suggest that the industrial revolution has destroyed empathy and so created a more uncaring and selfish society. This was a very common criticism of the age and, for example, is the most important theme in Charles Dickens' novel, *Hard Times*.

Thus it is possible, at least on a subconscious level, that Wells's Martian invasion may also be symbolic of his perception of the profound psychological damage caused by industrialisation which, if not controlled, alienates man from man and ultimately dehumanises society. Consequently, men become monsters who prey on the weakness of those less empowered…rather like Wells's Martian invaders prey upon the human race.

Is *The War of the Worlds* still relevant today?

It certainly had retained considerable force, some forty years after it had first been published, when in 1938 Orson Welles capitalised on the international tension just prior to the Second World War to produce a radio version of the novel which was broadcast as if it was a series of live news bulletins about a real Martian invasion. Newspapers of the time reported a resulting mass panic, although later historical research has since shown that this supposed general hysteria had been greatly exaggerated.

Today, unlike the period when the novel was written, our society provides a welfare state with all the benefits of a state education system, a national health service, social security, old age pensions, universal suffrage and legal equality. It might be argued that discrimination on the basis of social class is also, to some extent, a thing of the past.

However, the human race is still dealing with such fundamental issues as genocide, war, famine, poverty and human rights. The problems associated with rapid technological advance, which Carlyle had noted early on in the nineteenth century, have since become a recurrent theme in all societies. In this respect, the novel may well prove to be timeless.

GRADE *FOCUS*

Knowing how the culture and society of the day influenced an author will raise your grade, but interrupting your literature examination with a mini history essay will not.

Grade 8

Students should 'show perceptive understanding of how contexts shape texts and responses to texts', that is, identify and comment on the impact of the social, cultural and historical background of texts on different readers at different times.

Grade 5

Students should 'use understanding of contexts to inform responses to texts', that is, show some awareness of the social, cultural and historical background of texts and of how this influences their meanings.

The emphasis is on using the background historical information in order to better understand the text and thus better analyse the novel's probable impact on the reader, although a modern reader of *The War of the Worlds* will most likely react in a different manner to a Victorian reader. Similarly, fear of invasion by a powerful foe possessing vastly superior fire power may not be especially relevant to readers in the United Kingdom of today, but it would certainly strike a chord in certain parts of Eastern Europe, the Middle East and many other parts of the world.

REVIEW YOUR LEARNING

(Answers are given on p. 101.)

1 During which years did H. G. Wells live?

2 How might Wells's personal circumstances have affected the subplot with the curate?

3 In what ways does Wells's novel appear to have been influenced by the work of Thomas Carlyle?

4 What was the title of Percival Lowell's 1895 supposedly scientific book which clearly influenced Wells's description of the Martians' plight in Chapter 1 of his novel?

5 In what ways does the novel appear to have been influenced by Wells's understanding of Darwin's theory of evolution?

6 What does the novel suggest about the British Empire?

7 Through his presentation of the Martians, what might Wells be suggesting about the industrial revolution?

8 In what ways is *The War of the Worlds* still relevant today?

Target your thinking

- When and where is *The War of the Worlds* set? (**AO3**)
- What are the main events of the novel and when do they occur? (**AO1**)
- Why does Wells frequently shift narrative perspective within the novel? (**AO2**)
- How does Wells continually create suspense and excitement? (**AO2**)
- Where in the novel does the focus begin to change towards a psychological narrative? (**AO2**)

Form

The War of the Worlds is divided into two books and each book purports to recount a different phase of the Martian invasion. Book 1, *The Coming of the Martians*, recounts how the Martians arrive on Earth and then quickly take over London and the surrounding countryside. It provides highly descriptive panoramic accounts of the ferocious Martian advance and the brave but frequently unsuccessful attempts of the British military to halt them. Wells also has the narrator describe in tremendous detail the consequent fear-fuelled evacuation of people northwards and to the Essex coast.

Book 2 purports to detail life on Earth under Martian rule, but this is mainly from the very restricted view that Wells gives the first person narrator via the peephole overlooking the fifth cylinder which has crashed right next to the house in Sheen. Furthermore, as the Martians succumb to earthly bacteria sometime in the third week of the invasion, and as the Martians seem to have been largely located to London and its environs, Book 2 does not really live up to its grandiose title of *The Earth Under the Martians*. It would live up to the lesser title of 'London and Suburbs Fleetingly Under Martian Control'.

The novel was originally published as an illustrated monthly serial between April and December 1897 in the London-based *Pearson's Magazine* and in New York's *Cosmopolitan* magazine. As a result, the form of the novel may well have impacted on the structure, in the sense that Wells frequently recaps the same events both from the narrator's perspective and from that of another character (mainly the younger brother) who has since related his story to the narrator, thus enabling Wells regularly to refresh the magazine reader's memory.

Furthermore, the serialisation form will also have influenced the structure of the novel in that it required Wells to generate considerable suspense throughout the novel so as to encourage readers to keep buying the next instalment.

Build critical skills

Think about the ways in which high-profile sci-fi television shows or films such as *12 Monkeys* and *Extant* create, satisfy and then recreate new strands of suspense so as to maintain ratings. Now chart the progress of one line of suspense in *The War of the Worlds*. Do the points of climax always appear at the end of a chapter or volume?

Setting

The events which take place in the novel are set in a very defined location and are not, as the novel's dramatic title would suggest, global. Wells uses real place names, which definitely adds impact to the supposed 'realism' of the account, and the locale he uses is mainly the suburbs of London and London itself. At the time of writing the novel, Wells was living in 143 Maybury Road in the eastern part of the town of Woking, Surrey, a distance of approximately thirty miles south-west of London. Of course, this is exactly where Wells's narrator lives.

In order to gather inspiration for his most detailed scenic descriptions, Wells actually cycled round the area, presumably taking notes, and jokingly remarked in a letter sent to a friend, Elizabeth Healey:

> I'm doing the dearest little serial for Pearson's new magazine, in which I completely wreck and destroy Woking — killing my neighbours in painful and eccentric ways — then proceed via Kingston and Richmond to London, which I sack, selecting South Kensington for feats of peculiar atrocity.

Time frame

In the opening paragraph of the novel, Wells has the narrator addressing the reader from some unspecified point in the future, which is evidently post-1900, and referring back to a Martian invasion which took place six years earlier: 'early in the twentieth century came the great disillusionment'.

The narrator also informs us that during the opposition of 1894, and 'the next two oppositions', intense light could be observed emanating from the Martian surface which, he conjectures, was most likely 'the casting of the huge gun', that being the method of propulsion by which the Martians would ultimately launch their invasion force. Historically speaking, the two subsequent oppositions that he is referring to here were 1896 and 1899. The one after that was due to occur in 1901, so that could possibly be the year that Wells had in mind for the invasion, in which case the narrator would be speaking to us from 1907.

Constructing an exact time line of events within the novel, especially for Book 2, is complicated by the fact that Wells often doesn't mention days of the week and neither is he particularly consistent with regard to the passage of time. For example, in Book 2, Chapter 7, the narrator refers to having been trapped in the house in Sheen for 'thirteen or fourteen days' (p. 151) and yet in Book 2, Chapter 5 (on p. 142), he refers to having been there on a 'fifteenth day'.

Much of the timeline for Book 2 which follows is based on the fact that the narrator and the curate move into the house at Sheen late on a Monday evening and the assumption that when Wells has the narrator refer to the number of days spent in the house, which he does at various times during Book 2, the following day (Tuesday) constitutes the first full day of 'imprisonment'. Therefore, all references to specific days of the week after that Monday which appear in this section of the guide are close guesstimates.

By the end of the novel, Wells's time structure makes perfect sense when in Book 2, Chapter 9, he has the narrator finally arrive home again and describe the time since the Friday when the cylinder had landed on Horsell Common as 'scarcely a month gone by' (p. 176). Thus the arrival of the Martians in the skies above the southeast England to the time of the narrator returning home and being reunited with his wife is approximately 28 days.

As to the time of year, the various mentions of the sweltering weather suggest that it is midsummer and, at the beginning of Book 1, Chapter 17, Wells has his narrator refer to it being June.

Book 1: The Coming of the Martians

Chapter 1: The Eve of the War

- The narrator addresses the reader from some point after 1900.
- He is referring back to a Martian invasion of the Earth which took place six years before, 'early in the twentieth century...'
- Mars is a dying planet and so the highly advanced Martians intend to colonise the Earth.
- They send an invasion force of ten craft which they launch by means of a 'huge gun', probably some sort of massive cannon.
- The Martians invade when Mars is at its closest to earth, a mere 35 million miles away.

The novel is off to a blistering start, with enormous suspense being generated by the opening 'prologue' in which Wells has the narrator inform the reader that the invasion has already taken place. The reader is immediately beset by many questions. What form did the invasion take? What do the Martians look like? Are they in control of the Earth at the time that the narrator is speaking to us? Are there many humans still left alive? Or, more frighteningly, is the narrator a lone voice?

Accompanied by the vivid descriptions of the dying planet Mars, which Wells beautifully contrasts with the vibrant Earth, a powerful impact is created upon the imagination which propels the reader right into the fictional world of the novel. Furthermore, the various philosophical speculations about the nature of life and man imbue the writing with a dark grandeur and so help create the impression that this is far more than just a mere work of fiction.

GRADE BOOSTER

Action, suspense, vivid description and philosophical speculation are vital aspects of Wells's craft. He is more focused on these than he is on character development as we might, for example, find in the novels of his contemporary, Thomas Hardy. You might refer to this in an examination response about one of the major characters.

Build critical skills

For the power of Wells's intense word-painting, re-read the contrasting descriptions of Mars and Earth (p. 8). How vividly do they convey impressions of the abundance of Earth and the deficiency of Mars? Note the amount of explicit detail in both these 'word vistas'. Wells's writing is often intensely poetic and stunningly beautiful.

Chapter 2: The Falling Star (Week 1 of the Martian invasion begins)

- The first cylinder falls on Horsell Common in the very early hours of Friday morning.
- A shocked Ogilvy is the first to visit it around dawn.
- Initially, his account of the alien craft is met with disbelief by locals.
- He returns a little later that morning with a journalist called Henderson.

Henderson wires the astounding news to his newspaper in London. One way in which Wells overcomes the limitations of the first person narrator is by relaying the reported accounts of other characters to the reader via the narrator. However, in this instance, Wells is playing a clever trick on the reader as it is extremely unclear when Ogilvy would have had time to send the narrator so much information about the cylinder as Ogilvy has a very busy day and is killed in the evening!

It is heavily ironic that it is Ogilvy who makes the discovery, as Wells has made Ogilvy's disbelief in the existence of Martians clear in Chapter 1. This irony helps to enhance the dramatic impact of the scene upon the reader. Wells has also added notable tension as a result of the eerie stillness of the morning, which suggests the extra-terrestrial nature of the cylinder, and which **dramatically foreshadows** its lurking menace.

There is also an element of humour in the chapter as the incredulous locals fail to believe Ogilvy, and treat him as if he is 'a lunatic at large' (p. 15).

dramatic foreshadowing: when minor details are included to prepare the reader for much more momentous events to come. Dramatic foreshadowing can be used to build suspense or to make these later events seem more credible.

GRADE BOOSTER

As the novel was initially released in serialised form, it was essential that Wells regularly maintain suspense. Showing the examiner a relevant awareness of how the form of a text impacts upon the content will definitely help to improve your grade.

Key quotation

He did not remember hearing any birds that morning, there was certainly no breeze stirring, and the only sounds were the faint movements from within the cindery cylinder. He was all alone on the common.
(p. 14)

Chapter 3: On Horsell Common

- The narrator visits the cylinder shortly after 8.45 a.m. the same Friday.
- He stops some boys throwing stones at it.
- When he returns again later in the day, he sees that the crowd has swelled significantly.
- A carnival atmosphere has now developed.
- The local authorities deem it necessary to control the crowd's access to the site.

The casual indifference of some of the onlookers and the subsequent carnival atmosphere do seem somewhat incongruous and unlikely in the face of such a potentially overwhelming event. However, they do allow Wells to create a false sense of security and so play to the ongoing dramatic irony, which is that we as readers are well aware of the tremendous danger of which the unconcerned and the curious crowd is so ignorant. Also, Wells deliberately maintains suspense with little details such as the almost casual reference to possible noises within the craft, a device which he had also used in Chapter 2.

Wells creates further interest by the fact that the crowd consists of all strata of society, thus reinforcing the significance of the event. This is the first very subtle indication of how the Martian invasion might have the effect of creating a more united humanity.

Key quotation

...a faint stirring was occasionally still audible within the case...
(p. 19)

Chapter 4: The Cylinder Opens

- The narrator returns at sunset on the same Friday and the crowd has grown to 'two or three hundred'.
- The crowd jostles nervously as a result of signs of activity from the cylinder.
- In the commotion, a 'shopman' falls into the Martians' pit.
- The cylinder opens and snake-like tentacles emerge, throwing the crowd into a panic.
- The terrified crowd withdraws to observe from a cluster of trees which is at a safer distance.

Wells initially creates tension with the seemingly casual detail of a boy running, terrified by the fact that the craft appears to be opening. Once the Martians appear, Wells then uses the reaction of the crowd as a means of reinforcing his description of how terrifying they are.

Build critical skills

The carefully crafted description of the Martians deliberately likens them to well-established images of fear and disgust. Re-read the relevant pages of the chapter and see if you can find three examples for each of these categories.

Oddly, the description of the Martians as they flounder around the pit is potentially absurd, and it makes them sound primeval and less evolved — not more evolved — than humans.

Chapter 5: The Heat-Ray

- Friday evening, as daylight is fading, the crowd of onlookers has enlarged as fascination has overcome fear.
- The Deputation, which includes Stent, Henderson and Ogilvy, approaches the pit waving a white flag of peace.
- The Martians fire their Heat-Rays, killing both the Deputation and a number of people in the crowd.

The chapter opens with the narrative device of establishing that the narrator's fascination with the appearance of the grotesque-looking

Martians has overcome his fear. This is useful in a first person narrative as it is more straightforward for the author if the narrator can be present in order to record events. Wells uses the crowd to normalise the narrator's behaviour: 'Evidently they shared my mental conflict' (p. 24).

It is only after the Martians have opened fire that Wells finally allows the narrator (and the crowd) to be so overcome with terror that they flee the scene in a panic.

Chapter 6: The Heat-Ray in the Chobham Road

- '... nearly forty people', including the Deputation, were killed by the Heat-Ray.
- The crowd had swelled up again to around 300 at the time of the 'massacre'.
- Ironically, Stent and Ogilvy had sent for soldiers 'to protect these strange creatures from violence' (p.29).
- As the crowd flee in horror, more people die in the crush to escape.

This chapter recounts the events of the massacre again and so the time is as above, 8.30 p.m. and after sunset on the Friday evening, but the narrator also presents a more general overview of events in the area that he could not have witnessed. Wells disguises this with such phrases as 'You may imagine…' or 'You may figure to yourself…' (p. 28).

From personal observation, the narrator informs the reader that more of the onlookers would have been killed had they not been sheltered by 'a hummock of heathery sand'. The Martians are clearly indiscriminate in their violence.

Wells is a master of vivid description; it is definitely one of the qualities which make him such a great writer. His depiction of the sharply defined edges of the concentrated Heat-Ray brilliantly conjures up the impression of what we today would call a laser beam.

Chapter 7: How I Reached Home

- Late that Friday evening, the narrator staggers home.
- On the way he meets some locals who anger him by their inability to see the danger posed by the Martians.

- Over a late dinner with his wife, he informs her of what has happened.
- He tries to reassure her, stating that the Martians will not be able climb out of their pit because of Earth's powerful gravity.
- In an aside to the reader, he admits that this generally held belief overlooked the Martians' technological expertise

Much of the narrator's behaviour in this chapter seems unlikely given the situation that he is in, because it lacks the urgency and panic that one would expect after such an ordeal. Wells clearly recognises this as he supplies a number of justifications for it, e.g. the narrator's detached nature, his trauma, and his mistaken belief that the aliens cannot get out of the pit, which he then qualifies further as 'the general opinion' (p. 33), citing two highly influential newspapers in order to 'prove' the point.

Build critical skills

Is it stretching credibility too far for Wells to ask the reader to believe that so much of educated society would really be so blasé and so unimaginative as to think that the Martians wouldn't be able to get out of a ditch? After all, they have mastered interplanetary space flight! Or is Wells making a point about humanity's complacency and lack of vision? What do you think?

The chapter ends with a nice touch of dramatic foreshadowing about that being 'the last civilized dinner' he would eat for 'very many strange and terrible days'.

Chapter 8: Friday Night

- England carries on as normal and people 'talked about it in their leisure'.
- However, the people around the edge of Horsell Common are much less complacent, being 'kept awake till dawn'.
- The Martians are busily 'hammering' through the night, making machines.
- And the military authorities are certainly taking the situation seriously as soldiers have been dispatched to form a cordon around Horsell Common.

Again, Wells has his first person narrator provide a wider point of view, as if he is writing a history book, and this time he reports the Friday evening that he has already described in great detail in the preceding chapters from a more national perspective. The chapter ends dramatically with the suspense-fuelled statement that the second cylinder fell 'a few seconds after midnight' (very early Saturday morning).

Chapter 9: The Fighting Begins

- On Saturday morning, the day begins with surprising normality: the milkman arrives and the narrator's neighbour gives him some strawberries.
- In the afternoon and early evening, the military unsuccessfully attack the first two cylinders.
- About 6 p.m., the Martians respond with their Heat-Rays.
- The Heat-Rays cause mass destruction to the surrounding area and buildings.
- The narrator finally realises that he needs to evacuate his wife to Leatherhead.

Key quotation

The sun, shining through the smoke that drove up from the tops of the trees, seemed blood-red...
(p. 41)

The blood-red sun could be suggestive of the blood red moon in the Book of Revelation in which the Apocalypse, the end of the world, is foretold. (See 'Thomas Carlyle and the politics of the Apocalypse' in the 'Context' section of this guide.) However, it could also be seen as a symbol of the domination of the blood-drinking invaders from the Red Planet.

Chapter 10: In the Storm

- It is Saturday evening and the narrator sets out on the return journey from Leatherhead to Maybury just before 11 p.m.
- On the way, he sees a third cylinder fall.
- At Maybury, he has a terrifying encounter with a Martian tripod.

Mention of the third cylinder ratchets up the suspense and helps to create a sense of the overwhelming power of the Martian force. The backdrop of the storm is a perfect metaphor for the enormous conflict taking place on the ground and so further helps to ratchet up the tension. It also might be seen to reflect the Book of Revelation, as exactly the same type of violent storm takes place there too.

Chapter 11: At the window

- In the early hours of Sunday morning, the narrator arrives home dishevelled and traumatised.
- He spots a soldier in his garden to whom he offers shelter.

▲ Martian tripods (illustration by Henrique Alvim-Corrêa)

- The artilleryman gives an account of his unit's unsuccessful battle with the Martians on Saturday evening.
- The two men talk till dawn.

This is another good example of Wells extending the limitations of the first person narrator, as a good part of the chapter involves the narrator relating the artilleryman's account of the battle with the Martians. The narrator, of course, did not witness this battle for himself.

Wells ends the chapter with another biblical reference, this time to Exodus, thus continuing the religious framework of an apocalyptic scenario: 'Beyond were the pillars of fire about Chobham' (p. 55). Just as in Exodus, when the mighty Egyptians had tried to hunt down the fleeing Israelites, so are the humans fleeing from the mighty Martians. The reference is most appropriate as the mass exodus (escape) from London and the surrounding area takes up a big chunk of the end of Book 1. Also, the image symbolically foreshadows the novel's conclusion in that it implies that God is ultimately on the side of the afflicted human race.

Chapter 12: What I Saw of the Destruction of Weybridge and Shepperton

- At dawn on Sunday, the Narrator and the artilleryman vacate the narrator's house.
- The narrator intends to head for Leatherhead to rejoin his wife.
- The artilleryman intends to rejoin his military unit and resume the fight.
- The narrator gets diverted when he encounters a battle between five Martian tripods and concealed artillery units.
- The narrator takes cover in the River Thames.
- The tripods wreak tremendous destruction on the surrounding area.
- One of the tripods is unexpectedly destroyed, killing the Martian inside.

The river becomes scalding hot and the narrator staggers to the bank where he is almost crushed by one of the retreating tripods carrying off their fallen comrade.

This chapter is classic adventure story and is what Wells excels at best: fast-moving events with masses of action, an exciting battle scene, a panoramic overview (despite being a first person narrative), masses of multi-sensory description, for example, the vivid description of the scalding water, and the additional excitement of the highly unexpected event of a Martian tripod being destroyed. Much suspense is created by this latter event as it suggests that humanity has a chance and, therefore, that the Martian victory might not be inevitable. Historically speaking,

GRADE BOOSTER

Continuing the apocalyptic theme, the title of this chapter is a deliberate reference to another significant biblical event, the destruction of Sodom and Gomorrah, two cities situated on the River Jordan. In the Genesis story, these two cities were destroyed by God because of their sinful inhabitants. An examiner will be impressed by a candidate who can display such relevant biblical knowledge.

Key quotation

'It's bows and arrows against the lightning, anyhow,' said the artilleryman.
(p. 59)

it is also a nice jingoist touch as it renders a great compliment to the prowess of the British army.

Owing to the power of Wells's imagination, the novel is jam-packed with truly surprising events that the reader could never predict. This is one of the key qualities as to why it is such an exciting read and as to why it has become a classic.

Also note Wells's skill in depicting mass panic, a skill which he makes full use of as the novel progresses. In many respects, Wells is much more accomplished at writing crowd behaviour than he is at portraying individual psychology.

Chapter 13: How I Fell in with the Curate

- The Martians retreat to their original position on Horsell Common.
- Every twenty-four hours brings a new cylinder.
- Meanwhile, the military encircles an area of as much as twenty square miles around the pit at Horsell Common.
- Sometime after 4 or 5 p.m. that Sunday afternoon the sunburnt, dehydrated, exhausted and semi-delirious narrator has to temporarily stop his journey to rest.
- When he awakes, he finds the curate quietly observing him.
- The narrator is drawn into a deep theological and philosophical discussion about the meaning of the invasion and the nature of God.

Key quotation

'The smoke of her burning goeth up for ever and ever!' he shouted.
The curate (p. 70)

After the overwhelming pace of the last chapter, Wells provides a much-needed more static scene in order to allow the reader a chance to recover. The main interest now is in the philosophical discussion between the two men rather than in action. The curate cites a number of references from The Book of Revelation and clearly regards the invasion as the Apocalypse, God's punishment of the human race for its evil-doing. Equally, it might also be a reflection of the guilt he later reveals for not preaching against the great inequality in Victorian society.

Chapter 14: In London

- Takes place from Saturday morning to dawn Monday morning.
- An account of the Martian march towards London from the narrator's younger brother's point of view.
- It recounts the gradually emerging panic in London and the beginning of the scramble to escape the capital.
- It ends with the frantic Monday morning mass exodus of London as terrified crowds try to flee the capital.

In this chapter, there is a subtle time shift from the recent past to a point in the future one day ahead of where we last saw the narrator (which was Sunday). This is the first in a series of chapters in which Wells cleverly bypasses the limitations of the first person narrator by recounting events, which the narrator could not possibly have witnessed, from the point of view of his younger brother, a medical student in London. Two of the most obvious indications that the younger brother is little more than a narrative device are the fact that his personality is not greatly individualised from that of the narrator himself and the fact that Wells does not even bother to contrive to have the two meet up once the invasion is over!

Chapter 15: What had Happened in Surrey

- Time shifts back to Sunday night around 8 p.m.
- The chapter ends at just before dawn on Monday.
- As the narrator and the curate watch from their hiding place, seven Martian tripods form a huge crescent of twelve miles wide about their cylinders.
- The Martians return fire at the artillery using 'Black Smoke', a kind of poison gas.
- The narrator and curate shelter in a deserted house in Upper Halliford to avoid the Black Smoke.
- Sunday night sees the end of organised opposition against the Martians, the poison gas being the deciding factor.
- Before dawn on Monday, the British government is on the point of collapse and the exodus from London has begun.

This chapter returns to the narrator's perspective and fills in the details of the Martian advance upon London which Wells had deliberately shrouded in mystery in the previous chapter. In so doing, Wells brilliantly satisfies the suspense he had created through the narrator's brother's imperfect vantage point from inside London. Towards the end of the chapter, the first person narrator once again takes on a panoramic and omniscient perspective. He is able to do this owing to the fact that he is speaking with hindsight as he is addressing us from the future.

Key quotation

The whole population of the great six-million city was stirring, slipping, running; presently it would be pouring en masse northward.
(p. 82)

Key quotation

Before dawn the black vapour was pouring through the streets of Richmond, and the disintegrating organism of government was, with a last expiring effort, rousing the population of London to the necessity of flight.
(p. 91)

Chapter 16: The Exodus from London

- Takes place from dawn, Monday morning till Monday night.
- A return to the younger brother's point of view as he battles within the general exodus to escape London.

- En route, he saves two women, a Miss and Mrs Elphinstone, who are being attacked by three thugs.

The biblical Book of Exodus recounts the escape of the Israelites from slavery in Egypt. Wells has already made use of this reference before in Chapter 11 and may be implicitly suggesting that slavery is one of the horrors facing humanity under Martian rule.

▲ The Martians attacking a city, in the 1953 film

Wells brilliantly describes people of all classes getting caught up in this terrifying mass exodus from London. One way he does this is through his use of precise visual detail, e.g. the reference to the cart wheels being 'splashed with fresh blood' (p. 99). It is a most vivid and concise way of portraying the tremendous peril to pedestrians from vehicles as a result of the jam-packed main routes out of London.

Wells also intensifies the horror of the evacuation by zooming in on individual stories, e.g. the man who drops his sovereigns and gets his back broken trying to retrieve them and the sickly Chief Justice, Lord Garrick. It is thus made abundantly clear that neither wealth nor high office can save anyone from the Martians.

Notice also Wells's use of metaphorical language in order to magnify the terror of the experience. The chapter opens with the powerful metaphor of 'the roaring wave of fear' to express the crowd hysteria (p. 92). This imagery pattern runs throughout the chapter and emphasises both the irresistible onward movement of the crowd and the danger posed to the weaker members as they struggle to stay afloat in this powerful 'tide' of

Key quotation

It was the beginning of the rout of civilization, of the massacre of mankind.
(Book 1, Ch. 17, p. 104)

fleeing humanity. The image could be seen as appropriate as during the Israelites' exodus from Egypt, the waters of the Red Sea parted for them.

Build critical skills

Brian Aldiss, in his introduction to the Penguin Classics edition of the novel, quotes the entire second paragraph of this chapter, commenting: 'When it comes to the exodus from London, Wells's fear of the fragility of civilization and his dislike of the masses is again in evidence.' Re-read the paragraph yourself and make a note of what evidence there is here that law and order is collapsing.

Build critical skills

Re-read the whole of Chapter 16 and see how many references to water you can find. What effects are created by these references?

Chapter 17: The 'Thunder Child'

- Begins on Monday and ends Wednesday twilight.
- A continuation of the frantic exodus from London.
- The surviving half of the British government has relocated to Birmingham.
- The narrator's brother and his party of the Elphinstones head for the Essex coast.
- There is a huge naval battle between the British vessel *Thunder Child* and the Martian tripods which are threatening the shipping, and this results in at least two of the tripods being destroyed and the probable loss of the *Thunder Child*.
- At this point, the narrator's brother and his two companions are able to escape abroad on a steamboat.
- The falling of the fifth, sixth and seventh cylinders is also mentioned in this chapter.

This is the last time we hear of the narrator's brother, but we can safely assume that he and his party successfully escape abroad as the narrator is able to tell us their story. Seemingly, Wells no longer had need of this method of extending the first person narrative perspective as the brother is never mentioned again.

Wells ends the chapter, and Book 1, with yet another terrifying image which alludes to a biblical reference: 'And as it flew it rained down darkness upon the land.' (p. 112), which compares with '... there was a thick darkness in all the land of Egypt' (Exodus 10:22).

This closing line, which seemingly refers to some cataclysmic Martian flying machine, also generates tremendous suspense, thus encouraging the reader to continue on into Book 2. The machine itself is a loose end which Wells never really develops, however, it does predict the aerial bombing of the First World War.

Book 2: The Earth Under the Martians

Chapter 1: Under Foot

- The narrator relates events from his point of view during the period Sunday night to Tuesday night.
- The narrator and the curate shelter from the Black Smoke in the house at Halliford on Sunday night and all day on the Monday until about 5 p.m.
- Sometime after 8.30 p.m. as they make their way towards Sheen, they observe a Martian tripod near Kew collecting humans (as we later find out) for food and so the two men hide in a ditch until nightfall.
- It is between 11 p.m. and midnight on that Monday night when they move into the house in Sheen.
- Just before midnight, the house is reduced to rubble by the falling of the fifth cylinder.

In this chapter, Wells introduces another unusual narrative technique which is the device of the convenient 'gap in the wall' (pp. 120–121) which allows the narrator to make observations of the Martian pit below.

Mary Shelley uses a very similar technique in Volume 2 of her classic sci-fi horror story *Frankenstein*, published in 1818, in which the monster spends months secretly observing a family through a hole in the dividing wall between the hovel where he is hiding and the main cabin where the family lives.

This chapter is further significant in that there is a notable change in the tempo of the novel which slows down markedly in terms of action as Wells places far more focus on the developing subplot between the narrator and the curate.

Chapter 2: What We Saw from the Ruined House

- On Tuesday, the first day of 'imprisonment' in the house, the narrator provides a very detailed description of activity within the Martian pit.
- In particular, he is extremely impressed with the great dexterity of the spider-like handling-machine and reflects how later study of it has greatly advanced human technology.
- He also provides a very detailed anatomical description of the Martians.
- He describes how the Martians inject the blood of living humans directly into their veins.

The vampire-like blood-injecting of the Martians may well owe something to Bram Stoker's *Dracula* which was published in May 1897 at the same time as *The War of the Worlds* was being serialised. Certainly,

Wells is going full out to ratchet up the horror in an attempt to both shock and excite his readers.

Chapter 3: The Days of Imprisonment (the end of Week 1 and start of Week 2 of the Martian invasion)

- Takes place from Tuesday to Saturday, the first to the fifth day of imprisonment.
- There is growing tension between narrator and the curate, which frequently escalates into violence.
- The narrator tries to maintain a pragmatic and relatively rational response to the situation, whereas the curate's behaviour becomes increasingly irrational as he loses his faith.
- Consequently, the narrator's contempt for the curate intensifies as the days pass, especially as the curate resists all of the narrator's attempts to ration the dwindling food supply.
- Both men continue to observe the Martians and witness a man disappearing to his death on Tuesday and, on Thursday, even more horrific, the Martians feeding on a boy.

As well as providing more details about the Martians, this chapter continues the pronounced psychological narrative that Wells has begun to develop as he portrays the narrator's growing antipathy towards the curate. The suspense and tension here is as much about the deteriorating relationship between the two men as it is about the Martians.

> **GRADE BOOSTER**
>
> A psychological narrative is one which delves into a character's inner thoughts and feelings rather than recounting events. Some might argue that this is not one of Wells's strong points in this novel. Demonstrating such a deep critical awareness of Wells's style will impress the examiner.

Wells skilfully ends the chapter by reminding the reader of the external conflict which rages beyond the house when he has the narrator refer to hearing 'booming' artillery gun fire. Not only does this neatly maintain the reader's interest about the main subject of the novel, 'the war of the worlds', but it also provides an effective backdrop to the rapidly escalating friction between the two men within the house.

Chapter 4: The Death of the Curate

- Takes place from Sunday, the sixth day of imprisonment in the house, to Friday, the eleventh day.

- Friction over the curate's unwillingness to ration food continues until on the ninth day of their imprisonment, Wednesday, the narrator ends up striking the curate with a meat-chopper which leads to his death — although it is unclear whether the narrator's blow is the actual cause of death.
- The noise alerts the Martians, who probe into the house via the tentacles of a handling machine.
- The body of the curate is dragged off, presumably as food.
- Fearing discovery by the Martians, the narrator then hides in the coal cellar for the next couple of days, emerging again on the eleventh day.

This chapter is very reminiscent of the brooding, claustrophobic atmosphere of *Crime and Punishment,* written by Russian novelist Fyodor Dostoyevsky and first published in 1866. In Dostoyevsky's novel, dire circumstance pushes a fundamentally decent man into committing a brutal murder with the butt of an axe. The narrator's attack on the curate with the butt of a meat cleaver is justifiable as the latter seems to have been about to expose them both to the Martians.

▲ The death of the curate (illustration by Henrique Alvim-Corrêa)

protagonist: the main character in a work of fiction

However, Wells's narrator lacks the depth and complexity of psychological realism that we find in Dostoyevsky's work. Wells's **protagonist** certainly suffers no prolonged self-torturing pangs of conscience and remorse which might ultimately threaten to destroy him. In fact, the narrator is rather blasé about his crime. Wells's forte is brilliant description, breathtaking action and remarkable inventiveness rather than psychological realism.

Of course, you could argue that as Wells's narrator was far more justifiable in his actions than Dostoyevsky's protagonist, the striking of the curate clearly being an act of self-preservation, there is not the same requirement for such great angst.

Chapter 5: The Stillness (Week 3 of the Martian invasion begins)

- Takes place from Friday (the eleventh day of imprisonment) to Tuesday (the fifteenth day).
- On the eleventh day of imprisonment within the house at Sheen, the narrator emerges from the coal cellar where he has been hiding from the Martians.
- He survives without food and with only minimal water until the fifteenth day.
- The general 'stillness' encourages him to venture outside of the house.
- Much to his surprise, he discovers that the Martians have vacated the pit.

Having created this unexpected plot development, Wells is now able to bring his narrator back into the outside world once again where all of the main action is. Much suspense is created by the question of where the Martians have gone. The seemingly casual reference to 'a multitude of crows [which] hopped and fought over the skeletons of the dead the Martians had consumed...' (p. 142) is typical of Wells's skill at maintaining lines of tension, this one being how deadly the Martians are.

Chapter 6: The Work of Fifteen Days

- Takes place on Tuesday, a continuation from the last chapter.
- The narrator leaves Sheen and scavenges for food.
- As he does so, he notes how alien the landscape looks because of the Martian red weed which has rapidly spread.
- He arrives at Putney sometime after sunset.

The 'fifteen days' in the title of this chapter refers to the Martian impact on this part of England during the time the narrator was incarcerated inside the house. The chapter makes an enormously powerful impact through Wells's highly detailed descriptions of what has now become an alien landscape owing to the Martians' red weed.

The red weed is first mentioned in Book 2, Chapter 2. It is a species of edible plant which the Martians have brought with them and have harvested here on Earth. The rapidity of its spread is a further symbol of their impact upon our planet, and its failure to thrive is the first sign of their ultimate demise.

Note the contrast between areas of enormous devastation and totally unscathed properties. This frequent use of contrast is one of the ways in which Wells keeps his writing fresh and exciting.

Wells then brilliantly augments this stunning word-painting with the narrator's assumption that most of the population in Britain has been exterminated and so the Martians have now carried their war of conquest abroad. Again, enormous suspense has been generated.

> **GRADE** *BOOSTER*
>
> Contrast is when an author creates stimulus for the reader by deliberately juxtaposing opposites. Juxtaposition means the placing of opposites close together for effect. Wells uses this technique quite often so look out for it in the extract on your examination paper.

Chapter 7: The Man on Putney Hill

- Takes place from Tuesday to Wednesday, continuing on from the last chapter.
- The narrator finds some biscuits in an inn in Putney, where he stays the night, delighted to be sleeping in a bed.
- While at the inn, he feels a short-lived spasm of grief for 'the killing of the curate' (p. 148), though not guilt, as he feels justified in his action.
- Shortly after leaving the inn the next morning (Wednesday), he meets the artilleryman.
- He listens to the artilleryman's wild ideas about the future of humanity and his plans for survival as leader of a colony of strong, free humans who will live underground.
- The narrator quickly becomes disillusioned with the artilleryman and so leaves him in his house on Putney Hill and makes his way to London.

The main interest in this chapter lies in the artilleryman's extreme and highly unusual ideas of how the Martians will tame humanity once they conclude the war and then treat humans as farm animals, hunters and pets.

GRADE *BOOSTER*

```
In any response to the novel, be careful to
distinguish between the characters' views (including
the narrator's) and those of Wells himself. For
example, do not assume that the artilleryman's
beliefs are representative of Wells's own beliefs.
Recall that he distances himself from them with the
narrator's dismissal of the artilleryman as a 'strange
undisciplined dreamer of great things' (p.162).
```

Chapter 8: Dead London (Week 4 of the Martian invasion begins)

- The next day, Thursday, the narrator heads for London.
- He finds London depopulated.
- The wailing of one Martian echoes throughout the lifeless city.
- When the wailing stops, the narrator, unnerved by the sudden silence and by loneliness, hides away in a cabman's shelter for the rest of the evening.
- When he emerges before dawn the next morning, Friday, he sees another strangely still Martian tripod and, overcome by a sense of hopelessness, approaches it with suicidal intent.
- However, he discovers that the Martian inside has died.
- With a renewed sense of hope, he rushes towards the Martian base and finds 'nearly fifty' dead Martians in their huge pit.
- It is only much later that he discovers that this is because they had no immunity to Earth's bacteria.

This is another chapter which is notable for Wells's use of haunting, multisensory description as he conjures up a vivid impression of 'Dead London'. In particular, the dying Martian's cry of 'Ulla, ulla...' is most melancholy. There is also more convincing psychological complexity to the narrator in this chapter, for example, when he reacts with very credible distress at the sudden silence.

Furthermore, as we have seen so often before in the novel, Wells creates enormous interest, and frequent **irony**, through his continually unpredictable plot twists, this one being the destruction of the evolutionarily advanced Martian invaders by something as primordial as a microbe.

Build critical skills

Some readers find the Martians' child-like death wails oddly sympathetic. How do you feel?

irony: in this case, it means the opposite of what one might expect to happen

Chapter 9: Wreckage

- Takes place from Friday to Thursday of Week 4 of the Martian invasion.
- The narrator says he has no recollection of the next three days.

Key quotation

Across the Channel, across the Irish Sea, across the Atlantic, corn, bread, and meat were tearing to our relief. All the shipping in the world seemed going Londonward in those days.
(p. 172)

- However, during this period, news of the demise of the Martians has spread around the world and many nations are frantically sending supplies to London.
- On the Sunday, presumably his third day of wandering the London streets, the demented narrator is discovered by a kindly family ('these four-day friends') who shelter and protect him.
- The narrator then leaves to return home to Maybury after this period of four days, that possibly being on a Thursday.
- During the train journey out of London he notes the extent of the damage and the many signs of reconstruction already taking place.
- On arriving home he reflects upon how it is 'scarcely a month gone by' since the Friday when the first cylinder had landed.
- The chapter ends with an unexpected reunion with his wife.

Surprisingly, the trains are up and running very quickly after the Martian demise, thus indicating the great resilience of humanity.

The reunion between the narrator and his wife is a last-minute concession to the romantic novel which was so popular in the nineteenth century (and which still is!). Of course, romantic love is merely a subsidiary theme in this novel of large-scale action and adventure. Of more interest in this chapter is the first sign of a new and much more united world order.

Chapter 10: The Epilogue (the present day, six years on from the Martian invasion)

- From his study, the narrator reflects upon the impact of the Martian invasion on both the human race and himself.
- The Martians died because they had no natural immunity to Earth's bacteria.
- Although much of the Martian technology is still not understood, humanity has learned a great deal and thus made great scientific and technological advances.
- The invasion has also done much to promote 'the conception of the commonweal of mankind' (p. 179).
- However, the narrator fears that the human race is not being vigilant enough about the possibility of a second invasion.

utopia: an ideal place. The idea of creating such a society has long been a major theme in English literature.

Wells ends the novel with the **utopian** notion of a much more unified and morally elevated human race, possibly even anticipating our own United Nations as it struggles to make our world a better place.

The preserved Martian in the Natural History Museum is a nice touch of dark humour and greatly helps to restore the dignity of a battered humanity. The narrator's own concerns about the continuing security of the Earth provide a powerful cliffhanger of a conclusion which opens up the possibility of a sequel, had Wells wished to write one.

Wells had a keen interest in history and a possible historical parallel for the exhibited Martian is when the Persian king, Shapur (AD 210–272) supposedly had the captured Roman Emperor Valerian skinned, stuffed with straw, and then publically displayed in the main temple. The story appears in Edward Gibbon's *The History of the Decline and Fall of the Roman Empire*, a classic text first published in 1776. Gibbon comments 'The tale is moral and pathetic...' Wells's tale has a similarly moral and cautionary purpose, that being a warning against aggressive imperialism, both Martian and British!

GRADE *FOCUS*

When writing about *The War of the Worlds* in the exam, do not write long narrative accounts of what happens in the novel.

Grade 8
Students will be required to 'sustain a convincing, informed personal response to explicit and implicit meanings of texts'.

Grade 5
Students will be required to 'develop a generally coherent and engaged response to explicit and implicit meanings of texts'.

Neither of the above grades requires you to retell the story in your responses. As always, it is important to answer the question which is being asked.

REVIEW YOUR LEARNING

(Answers are given on p. 101.)

1 In which year did *The War of the Worlds* begin to be serialised?

2 What were the two main things which motivated Wells in his choice of Woking and the surrounding area as the setting for the novel?

3 When is most of the action in the novel set?

4 When is the narrator addressing us from?

5 Over what period of time does the main action span?

6 Why do the Martians launch their invasion when they do?

7 Why do the Martians invade?

8 What weapons do the Martians use?

9 What is the fatal weakness that dooms the Martian invasion?

Target your thinking

- What methods does Wells use to present his characters to the reader? (**AO2**)
- For what purposes does Wells use his characters? (**AO2**)

How Wells reveals character

The personality of a character can be revealed in a variety of ways:

- **Actions** — what a character does and how this affects other characters.
- **Dialogue** — what a character says and what other characters say about that character.
- **Thoughts** — the secret unexpressed hopes, desires and perceptions that a character may inwardly conceive but does not wish to divulge to other characters. In a first-person narrative like *The War of the Worlds* the narrator can only really have a detailed knowledge of his or her own thoughts and feelings, and these are being constantly revealed. Therefore, the reader is unlikely to tolerate too high a level of intuitive guesswork regarding the thoughts and feelings of other characters. Yet, Wells frequently has his narrator provide us with such information (especially concerning the thoughts and feelings of his younger brother) – even though such god-like omniscience (knowing everything) is more the preserve of a third-person narrator.
- The **narrator's observations** on the personality and behaviour of himself and other characters.
- **Description** — carefully chosen words and images to portray a character's personality.

The War of the Worlds is a first-person narrative and, therefore, the reader should be wary of taking all of the narrator's comments at face value. However, Wells is clearly presenting the unnamed narrator as an individual of considerable courage, rationality, intelligence, learning and integrity and, therefore, as somebody the reader can admire and trust.

The character studies that follow use evidence derived from all of the above ways in which Wells reveals his major characters to the reader.

The narrator

The narrator is Wells's main tool for conveying the story to the reader and, as such, some critics regard him as more of a narrative device than a

GRADE BOOSTER

When writing about character, it is important to show the examiner that you understand that characters are not real people but creations of the author which have been designed for such ulterior purposes as creating suspense, advancing plot and developing themes.

credible character in his own right. Such critics consider that his reactions to the situations in which Wells places him are not always particularly convincing. There are actually a number of occasions in the novel when Wells could be perceived as acknowledging this. One example is when he provides the narrator with a justification for not fleeing in terror when the Martians first appear out of the cylinder: 'I was a battleground of fear and curiosity' (Book 1, Ch. 5, p. 24).

If the narrator had followed normal human instinct and fled for his life then Wells would have had to find a roundabout way of telling us what happens next, as the narrator would not have been there to witness it. Furthermore, the narrator's character would appear much less heroic and, therefore, less admirable.

However, an alternative reading of the narrator might focus on the sci-fi genre and point out that his character is perfectly in accord with a style of writing in which action is generally given priority over psychological realism. Furthermore, the 'battleground of fear and curiosity' noted above does fit in with the notion of him being a scientist.

Build critical skills

There is quite a marked debate here regarding Wells's characterisation of the narrator. What do you think?

▲ Tom Cruise in the 2005 film

In the opening chapter, Wells quickly establishes the narrator's credentials for relating such a monumental episode in the history of humanity as the Martian invasion, when he has the narrator describe himself as being 'busy upon a series of papers discussing the probable developments of moral ideas as civilization progressed' (p. 12). This kind of academic status is essential for the narrator's reliability as an accurate reporter and commentator, especially as Wells uses the narrator to make many

The War of the Worlds

GRADE BOOSTER

In the examination, be careful not to assume that Wells's views are exactly the same as those held by the narrator.

Key quotation

Few people realize the immensity of vacancy in which the dust of the material universe swims.
(Book 1, Ch. 1, p. 10)

Key quotation

People in these latter times scarcely realize the abundance and enterprise of our nineteenth-century papers.
(Book 1, Ch. 1, p. 12)

interesting philosophical judgements on the nature of humanity and the universe during the course of the novel.

The narrator frequently uses a condescending tone and often presents himself as the common man's intellectual and moral superior, especially when Wells provides him with such phrases as 'Few people realize...' and 'People in these latter times scarcely realize...' However, Wells is careful to ensure that his narrator treats the reader as an equal so as not lose his audience's sympathy:

> The planet Mars, I scarcely need remind the reader, revolves about the sun at a mean distance of 140,000,000 miles...
>
> (Book 1, Ch. 1, p. 7)

The narrator also has a rather cynical view of human nature, as Wells indicates when the narrator reflects to himself 'I fancy the popular expectation of a heap of charred corpses was disappointed at this inanimate bulk' (Book 1, Ch. 3, p. 17). Admittedly, the narrator does hold more positive views about his fellow humans by the time of the final chapter when he informs us that the failed Martian invasion 'has done much to promote the conception of the commonweal of mankind' (p. 179). However, the tone is still moralistic and appraising and hence he is essentially a static character who exhibits no real personal growth.

The narrator's more attractive qualities are founded in a Victorian concept of rugged manliness with which Wells has imbued him for contemporary readers. He is a natural born leader as is shown in Book 1, Chapter 12 when he shouts for people to 'Get under water!' so as to avoid the Martian Heat-Ray. Although Wells qualifies this by having the narrator comment that his cry went 'unheeded', we are then informed that 'Others did the same' (p. 62). The narrator's forceful personality is also demonstrated by the way in which the curate slavishly follows him from place to place until they reach the house in Sheen.

Wells has also endowed the narrator with the admirable qualities of courage and integrity, such as when he risks his life to return the landlord's dog cart before midnight, as promised, and when he admits to the probable murdering of the curate despite, as he reminds the reader, not needing to open himself up to such potential condemnation as there were no witnesses. Equally, both of the above cases also illustrate his darker, more ruthless side: he deliberately withheld information about the Martian advance from the landlord so as to obtain the dogcart and he did bludgeon the curate in order to save himself from discovery by the Martians.

One critic has suggested that when Wells has the narrator state 'At times I suffer from the strangest sense of detachment from myself and the world about me...' (Book 1, Ch. 7, p. 32), he could almost be describing what we today would term as sociopathic tendencies. A sociopath is somebody who has a personality disorder which includes an absence of empathy and a lack of moral and social responsibility. Of course, Wells might simply have had him describe himself like this in order to explain his unusual reaction after the massacre on Horsell Common, that being returning home to have a cold dinner with his wife!

All of the characters in the novel are presented to us via the narrator's often very judgemental perspective. However, Wells does not allow the narrator to intrude upon the narrative to anywhere near the same extent when critiquing the younger brother's personality and, when he does so, his comments are always positive.

The narrator's younger brother

Just as with the narrator, some critics view him as more of a narrative device rather than a fully realised character. Wells uses him to extend the boundaries of the first person narrator to enable the narrator to report on the exodus from London from within the capital itself. The younger brother's lack of individuation is furthered by the obvious similarities between him and the narrator. For example, his natural terror is also overcome by 'fascination' when he is on board the steamer awaiting escape to Ostend.

This recalls the fact that the narrator was similarly 'paralysed' by the fascinating sight of the Martians emerging from the cylinder (Book 1, Ch. 5, p. 24).

As with the narrator, he is also presented as a stereotypical Victorian male, rugged and courageous, such as when he rescues Miss and Mrs Elphinstone from three ruffians. The kick which renders one of the thugs senseless demonstrates that he shares the narrator's inclination towards physical violence, when he thinks it necessary.

He also shares the narrator's compassionate nature, as is illustrated by him risking harm to attempt to save the injured man whose sovereigns mean more to him than his life and when he offers comfort to 'the little girl of eight or nine', separated from her mother (Book 1, Ch. 16, p. 100). Compare this with the narrator's sincere regret that he could not save the shopman who had fallen into the Martian pit in Book 1, Chapter 4.

Furthermore, as with the narrator, Wells presents the younger brother as a natural leader. He automatically assumes control of Miss and Mrs Elphinstone just as the narrator (reluctantly) assumes control of the curate. One difference, however, is that the younger brother does seem better able to protect the people under his care than the narrator who, of course, loses track of his wife and ends up killing the curate!

The curate

One of the main functions of the curate may well be to act as a representation of the hypocrisy of organised religion, but he is also the

> **Build critical skills**
>
> Does the narrator really fit the definition of a sociopath, or is he an essentially moral man struggling to survive under dire circumstances?

basis for Wells's subplot, i.e. the continual friction which exists between him and the narrator and which ultimately results in the narrator very possibly murdering him. In this sense, he is also used to suggest that during an invasion, even civilised men such as the narrator may be driven to extreme acts.

Wells begins his hostile presentation of the curate by immediately implying the curate's weakness of character through his rather feminine facial traits.

The language frequently used by Wells in the narrator's description of the curate creates an impression of a weak, selfish, undisciplined and unmanly character. Of course, in the context of this novel, being unmanly is a great condemnation, as Wells clearly admires the manliness in the narrator, the narrator's brother and the artilleryman.

One of the most obvious signs of the curate's weakness is his crisis of faith as a result of the invasion and his immediate assumption that God has abandoned the human race. The curate's feebleness in adversity can be interpreted as suggesting that organised Victorian religion is spiritually bankrupt and so immediately crumbles in the crisis.

Key quotation

'God have mercy upon us!'
I heard him presently whimpering to himself.
(Book 2, Ch. 1, p. 121)

Note how deliberately disparaging the word 'whimpering' is!

As the novel progresses, the narrator's criticisms of the curate become increasingly savage. In Book 2, Chapter 3, the narrator describes him 'as lacking in restraint as a silly woman' (p. 131), as 'this spoilt child of life' (p. 131) and as having 'sunk to the level of an animal' (p. 134).

Ultimately, however, Wells best condemns the curate through the curate's own actions, especially his selfish disregard of the narrator's sensible pleas to preserve the dwindling food supply when both men are trapped inside the house in Sheen and, in particular, through the curate's juvenile threat to make enough of a commotion to alert the Martians if he doesn't get his own way. So bestial, despicable and irrational has his behaviour become that Wells has created a scenario in which we can calmly accept his death at the hands of the narrator.

Build critical skills

Re-read the opening two pages of Book 2, Chapter 3, and make a note of at least five details where Wells seems to encourage the reader to despise the curate.

The artilleryman

The artilleryman first appears in Book 1, Chapter 11 and at this point Wells uses him as a means of informing the narrator, and hence the reader, about the unsuccessful attempt of the army to defeat the

Martians. Wells might well be aiming to present him as a brave soldier but the artilleryman's account of how he escaped death owing to an accident with his horse, which kept him out of much of the battle with the Martians, could create an element of doubt in a more cynical reader!

Key quotation
The Cardigan men had tried a rush, in skirmishing order, at the pit, simply to be swept out of existence.
(Book 1, Ch. 11, p. 53)

Build critical skills

Re-read the artilleryman's account of his role in the battle (pp. 53–54) as reported to us by the narrator and see what you think. The soldier's honesty about his terror is admirable, and he is clearly shell-shocked, but could he have played a more active role?

Although he initially appears to share the attributes of courage and resourcefulness that are so evident in both the narrator and his younger brother, Wells creates a distinctive persona for the artilleryman by nature of his profession as a soldier and by the fact that he is from the lower class. This is most effectively portrayed in the dialogue that Wells writes for him, a perfect example of which occurs in Book 1, Chapter 12 when the artilleryman describes a Martian tripod to a disbelieving officer:

'Giants in armour, sir. Hundred feet high. Three legs and a body like 'luminium, with a mighty great head in a hood, sir.'

(p. 58)

Each of the three statements is a fragment rather than a fully formed sentence and 'aluminium' has been abbreviated in order to recreate the artilleryman's lower-class pronunciation.

The artilleryman's professed desire to locate his unit and rejoin the fight against the Martians is admirable, as is his sound advice to the narrator about not heading directly towards Leatherhead as it would mean passing by the third cylinder. However, there is no actual evidence that he did resume battle and, for all we know, he may simply have gone into hiding. In Book 2, Chapter 7, he states 'After Weybridge I went south — thinking.' (p. 153) As he goes on to explain, he decided to plot his own course in search of a secure food supply and relative safety. But Wells also gives the artilleryman many brave and defiant words, and so the case is uncertain:

'I've been in sight of death once or twice; I'm not an ornamental soldier…'

(Book 2, Ch. 7, p. 153)

By the time the narrator meets up with him again in Book 2, Chapter 7, he has become quite the philosopher and is beginning to sound very like the narrator himself, so much so that the narrator is initially taken in by his extravagant ideas. Wells even has him using the narrator's previously expressed ant analogy.

GRADE BOOSTER

One way an author can reveal a character is not just through a character's words but through the way in which those words are expressed. Examiners will reward such a perceptive awareness of an author's craft.

Build critical skills

This ambiguity about the artilleryman could have been deliberately created, or it might be entirely unconscious. What do you think?

But the Martian machine took no more notice for the moment of the people running this way and that than a man would of the confusion of ants in a nest against which his foot has kicked.
The narrator (Book 1, Ch. 12, p. 63)

'This isn't a war,' said the artilleryman. 'It never was a war, any more than there's war between men and ants.'
(Book 2, Ch. 7, p. 152)

Build critical skills

Consider to what extent the artilleryman's obvious disdain for upper-class Victorian society is a reflection of Wells's own humble origins.

When in conversation with the narrator, Wells reveals the artilleryman's contempt for the deeply class-ridden Victorian society in which he is near the bottom of the heap:

'There won't be any more blessed concerts for a million years or so; there won't be any Royal Academy of Arts, and no nice little feeds at restaurants. If it's amusement you're after, I reckon the game is up. If you've got any drawing-room manners or a dislike to eating peas with a knife or dropping aitches, you'd better chuck 'em away. They ain't no further use.'

(Book 2, Ch. 7, p. 154)

The artilleryman's views here represent the post-invasion theme of self-preservation and the view that the thin Victorian veneer of manners and class rules no longer applies.

▲ British artillery entering enemy lines in Egypt, 1882

His dark vision of a subservient human race of farm stock, hunters of fellow humans and pets all living under Martian rule seems to play to the narrator's own cynical view of humanity at that time, and his vision of a race of strong men and women living freely beyond Martian control, which would include men of character and learning like the narrator, clearly appeals to the latter's vanity.

However, Wells purposely contrasts this vision of bold defiance with the futile task of building a redundant tunnel and the artilleryman's desire to cease work and relax well before the day's labour is finished. Consequently, the narrator (and, perforce, the reader) soon becomes disillusioned – and Wells can safely distance himself from some of the soldier's more radical and controversial ideas.

The game of euchre in which the artilleryman and the narrator divide up London between them is an example of Wells using symbolism to hint at the darker side of the artilleryman's nature. The artilleryman has already declared that he only wants people who 'obey orders', and thus Wells is creating the powerful suggestion that his real vision of an alternative human race is one of a tribal community which he will rule over as a kind of feudal chieftain.

As Wells is mainly allowing the reader to view the artilleryman through the prism of the narrator's own perceptions, then the reader is compelled to share the narrator's ultimate conclusion that the artilleryman has become a lesser man as a result of his recent traumas. (For more on the artilleryman, see pp. 55–56 of this guide.)

(For more on the artilleryman, see pp. 55–56 of this guide.)

GRADE *BOOSTER*

An author can use the thoughts of one character in order to undermine the standing of another character if that first character has already been presented as one that the reader should respect.

The Martians

Most of what we learn about the Martians is directly related to the reader via the first-hand experiences of the first person narrator who, as a result of his close-up observations of the Martians during the period of the invasion, is something of an expert. In the first chapter, we are informed that their reason for invading the Earth is based on the most fundamental of all motivations, the struggle to survive owing to the imminent death of their own planet. It is notable, however, that they make no attempt to share the Earth with human beings and, indeed, immediately destroy the Delegation with its white flag of peace.

As a result of the fact that Mars is much older than Earth, the Martians are far more intellectually, and hence scientifically and technologically, advanced than human beings. Not only are they capable of interplanetary space travel but, as the narrator tells us in the final chapter, their technology is so progressive that six years later people still cannot understand the workings of the Black Smoke and the Heat-Ray.

Key quotation

'Oh, one can't always work,' he said, and in a flash I saw the man plain.
(Book 2, Ch. 7, p. 159)

GRADE *BOOSTER*

Symbolism is a subliminal way of suggesting or reinforcing ideas to the reader about a character.

Key quotation

I resolved to leave this strange undisciplined dreamer of great things to his drink and gluttony, and to go on into London.
(Book 2, Ch. 7, p. 162)

Build critical skills

How the narrator has such a detailed knowledge of conditions on Mars is never explained to the reader. Do you think that Wells is overstretching the bounds of the first person narrator here?

Key quotation

*The immediate
pressure of necessity
has brightened their
intellects, enlarged
their powers, and
hardened their hearts.*
(Book 1, Ch. 1, p. 8)

Key quotation

*They have become
practically mere brains,
wearing different
bodies according to
their needs just as men
wear suits of clothes
and take a bicycle in a
hurry or an umbrella in
the wet.*
(Book 2, Ch. 2, p. 129)

Key quotation

*They seemed busy in
their pit, and there was
a sound of hammering
and an almost
continuous streamer of
smoke.*
(Book 1, Ch. 9, p. 40)

Key quotation

*It may be, on the
other hand, that the
destruction of the
Martians is only a
reprieve. To them, and
not to us, perhaps, is
the future ordained.*
(Book 2, Ch. 10, p. 179)

Wells's depiction of the Martians as highly advanced industrial artisans who work with hammers and fire and who smelt aluminium in order to make machines owes a great deal to the age in which the novel was written. At this time England was in a state of continual transformation as result of the ongoing industrial revolution which had begun over a hundred years earlier. The presentation of the Martians can also be seen as challenging the assumption held by many Victorians that the English were superior to all other races. So powerful is their technology that a very few Martians, just ten cylinders in all, are on the brink of defeating the entire human race.

Here, Wells appears to be influenced by real historical events. The Martian invasion of the Earth is very reminiscent of what happened in 1532 when a couple of hundred Spanish conquistadors led by Francisco Pizarro were able to set about destroying the mighty Inca nation, partly as a result of their superiority in weaponry. Wells even employs an image which compares the Martian Heat-Rays to swords:

> It was sweeping round swiftly and steadily, this flaming death, this invisible, inevitable sword of heat.
>
> (Book 1, Ch. 5, p. 26)

The Spanish victory was also heavily aided by the Incas' lack of immunity to the diseases that the conquistadors carried with them. The brilliant irony that Wells has created is that he makes the bacteriological factor work in reverse, this time killing the Martian invaders rather than the indigenous population, that being us! However, the end of the Martian threat to the human race is not assured: see Book 2, Chapter 10, p. 179.

In his physical depiction of the Martians, Wells seems to be influenced by a curious mixture of ancient mythology and Old Testament theology. The description of the Martians in Book 1, Chapter 4 describes 'the Gorgon groups of tentacles' (p. 22). In Greek mythology, the three Gorgons had writhing serpents protruding from their heads. The snake image might also be drawn from Genesis, the first book of the Bible, in which Satan corrupts Adam and Eve in the guise of a serpent. References to snakes recur at various points in the novel when describing both the Martians and their equipment. For example:

> Then something resembling a little grey snake, about the thickness of a walking-stick, coiled up out of the writhing middle...
>
> (Book 1, Ch. 4, p. 21)

Furthermore, the fact that the Martian base is referred to as a 'pit' possibly ties Wells's depiction of the Martians to the Bible, as in the Book of Revelation, the final book of the Bible, 'the beast' rises out a 'bottomless pit' in order to participate in the apocalyptic war which destroys the Earth. The smoke and fire which Wells constantly associates with the Martians also adds to this apocalyptic and satanic impression. In this sense, the Martians embody both supreme evil and represent a contemporary late-nineteenth-century concern about the end of the world as the next millennium (the twentieth century) loomed close.

For all these supernatural overtones, Wells is clearly using the Martians to characterise important aspects of society and human nature. In the opening chapter of the novel, their aggressive invasion is explicitly associated with British imperialism:

> And before we judge of them too harshly we must remember what ruthless and utter destruction our own species has wrought, not only upon animals, such as the vanished bison and the dodo, but upon its own inferior races.
>
> (p. 9)

And, of course, their overwhelming military superiority deliberately mirrors that of the British army when subduing less technologically advanced societies around the world.

Wells may also be using the Martians to expose the environmental damage and human misery caused by rapid industrialisation. The Martians are clearly characterised as brilliant mechanical engineers and are strongly associated with fire and smoke. Their hooting may well be derived from the factory hooters of the age. Moreover, they wreak havoc on the English countryside and ruthlessly destroy or exploit the local population.

For further insight into Wells's crucial characterisation of the Martians, see the 'Darwinian evolution', 'Millenarianism', 'Empire' and 'Industrialisation' parts of the 'Contexts' section of this guide and the 'Apocalypse', 'Nature of humanity' and 'Evolution' parts of the 'Themes' section of this guide.

REVIEW YOUR LEARNING

(Answers are given on p. 102.)

1 What six methods does Wells use to reveal his characters?

2 Which two characters are Wells's main narrative devices?

3 What might be the two main functions of the curate?

4 Most of Wells's characters are static characters, which means that they do not really develop or alter in any way. However, which character does show significant change, and how?

5 Which character is the reader least encouraged to sympathise with and why?

6 Which fundamental aspects of Victorian Britain might Wells be using the Martians to represent?

GRADE BOOSTER

Note how Wells is using imagery as a method of revealing his characters. When in the examination, be sure to refer to Wells's use of language whenever it is appropriate to do so.

GRADE FOCUS

How will you be assessed on character-based questions?

Grade 8
Answers will show perceptive insight into the nature of the characters and the author's methods for revealing aspects of character to the reader. There will be a sustained analysis of how authors use characters to advance the plot and, very often, to represent deeper purposes such as developing themes and presenting ideas.

Grade 5
Answers will demonstrate an understanding that characters are not real people but literary constructs and there will be a successful evaluation of some of the ways in which authors use characters to advance their purposes.

Target your thinking

- What is a theme? (**AO2**)
- What are the main themes in *The War of the Worlds*? (**AO2**)
- How do these themes relate to each other? (**AO2**)
- How do these themes relate to the characters? (**AO2**)

A theme is an idea that the author explores through such means as character, plot and language. Although the examination boards tend to set questions on either themes or characters, it is important to realise that this division is artificial. Characters, for example, are one method by which an author can develop themes. Here is a list of some of the more important themes in *The War of the Worlds*:

- the nature of humanity
- the Apocalypse
- imperialism
- war
- society
- evolution

The nature of humanity

It stands to reason that any text which presents an apocalyptic vision so directly must also include an evaluation of human nature and the moral failings that might have induced such a global disaster. In the opening chapter, Wells has the narrator sermonise:

> And before we judge of them [the Martians] too harshly we must remember what ruthless and utter destruction our own species has wrought, not only upon animals, such as the vanished bison and the dodo, but upon its own inferior races.
>
> (Book 1, Ch. 1, p. 9)

To reinforce the point, Wells then has his narrator explicitly reference the extermination of the indigenous population of Tasmania by British colonists earlier in the nineteenth century. Thus, the Martians are representative of man's own inhumanity to his fellow man.

At least until the novel's closing chapter when Wells refers to the developing 'commonweal of mankind', he presents humanity as being capable of great acts of heroism but, equally, as being a fundamentally primitive species which willingly exploits its fellow men for personal gain — and whose male offspring have to be restrained from throwing rocks at advanced alien space craft!

The Apocalypse

Through his narrative, Wells appears to tap into late Victorian society's fear of a final judgement upon the human race as the century (and the millennium) came to a close. This is made explicit in the novel when the curate declares:

'This must be the beginning of the end,' he said, interrupting me. 'The end! The great and terrible day of the Lord! When men shall call upon the mountains and the rocks to fall upon them and hide them - hide them from the face of Him that sitteth upon the throne!'

(Book 1, Ch. 13, p. 71)

▲ The biblical Apocalypse

The theme is continued when the curate delivers a telling social critique, claiming that the Martian invasion is God's punishment on humanity for having tolerated so much inequality.

To reinforce this overwhelmingly powerful and emotive theme, Wells inundates the novel with imagery drawn from the Book of Revelation. (See 'Thomas Carlyle and the politics of the Apocalypse' and 'Millenarianism' parts of the Context section in this guide.)

Key quotation

And we men, the creatures who inhabit this earth, must be to them at least as alien and lowly as are the monkeys and lemurs to us.
(Book 1, Ch. 1, p. 8)

Key quotation

'We have sinned, we have fallen short. There was poverty, sorrow; the poor were trodden in the dust, and I held my peace.'
The curate to the narrator
(Book 2, Ch. 4, p. 137)

In keeping with the biblical Apocalypse, Wells concludes the novel with his positive vision of a new and morally improved human race which arises out of the maelstrom of fiery destruction.

Imperialism

It is notable how Wells sets the invasion in the proximity of London, the centre of the then most powerful political and military entity in the world, the British Empire. It is clear from the opening chapter that Wells despises British imperialism and views it as being morally reprehensible because of its inherent exploitation and brutality, e.g. the reference to the 'extermination' of the Tasmanians. To this extent, the Martians are giving British imperialism a taste of its own medicine!

However, it is also patently obvious that Wells admires the British armed forces. Hence, the novel is full of heroic battles, such as when a Martian tripod is downed by British artillery in Book 1, Chapter 12, and when the naval warship, the *Thunder Child*, downs two, possibly three, tripods in Book 1, Chapter 17. Furthermore, there is a most revealing indication of Wells's patriotic pride when he has the narrator describe the Union Jack flying over the sixth cylinder in Book 2, Chapter 9.

War

There is a definite inbuilt ambivalence towards war within the novel. The novel can be read as a warning against the excesses of mechanised warfare. Wells uses his visionary genius in order to graphically portray how much more brutal war could become as military technology advanced and, in so doing, he predicts such First World War horrors as tanks, flame throwers and poison gas.

When Wells has the narrator declare, '...it certainly did not make the sensation that an ultimatum to Germany would have done' (Book 1, Ch. 8, p. 35), it is clear that tensions between Great Britain and Germany were very much to the fore at the time when the novel was written. Less than twenty years later, the First World War broke out and resulted in the deaths of many millions of people worldwide.

▲ The First World War: British front in Flanders, 1917

On the other hand, Wells has the narrator fatalistically suggest that war fever is an integral part of human nature and has the narrator caught up in the excitement of warfare on a number of occasions.

Towards the end of the novel, however, the great devastation and consequent war weariness has made the narrator suicidal. Therefore, it could equally be argued that rather than a celebration of the thrill of battle, the novel is really a sophisticated observation of a tragic historical cycle in which successive generations of men are initially excited by the idea of war until the horrific reality of combat teaches them wisdom.

Society

Perhaps much of the excitement at the idea of war which occurs in the novel is due to dissatisfaction with the status quo. Therefore, it may well be particularly meaningful that Wells uses the artilleryman to expose the meaninglessness of much of middle-class life in late Victorian society.

Key quotation

'They just used to skedaddle off to work — I've seen hundreds of 'em, bit of breakfast in hand, running wild and shining to catch their little season-ticket train, for fear they'd get dismissed if they didn't; working at businesses they were afraid to take the trouble to understand...Well, the Martians will just be a godsend to these.'
(Book 2, Ch. 7, p. 155)

Key quotation

For my own part, I had been feverishly excited all day. Something very like the war-fever that occasionally runs through a civilised community had got into my blood...
(Book 1, Ch. 10, p. 44)

Build critical skills

As Wells also has the narrator express disillusionment with the artilleryman by the end of the same chapter, to what extent can we assume that these ideas represent Wells's own thinking?

This expressed contempt for these timid office workers may well have been influenced by the depiction of the 'last man' in Friedrich Nietzsche's philosophical novel *Thus Spoke Zarathustra* (1883–1885). These 'last men' that Nietzsche warns of are mediocrities who are frightened of everything extreme or dangerous and so cling to an insignificant life of comfort and security. They are the antithesis of the 'overman', the strong-minded and charismatic individual so admired by Nietzsche, Thomas Carlyle and H. G. Wells himself. Nietzsche's 'overman' (*Übermensch* in German) possesses a unique insight through which he can reveal a more enlightened way of living to others. Of course, the artilleryman is a mere parody of this 'superman'.

Evolution

Darwin's theory of evolution is a huge influence on Wells and permeates the novel at various levels, including biological, technological and societal. As Wells makes clear in the opening chapter, the Martians are much more intellectually advanced than man because their planet is older and, therefore, their species has had longer to develop.

Key quotation

Yet across the gulf of space, minds that are to our minds as ours are to those of the beasts that perish, intellects vast and cool and unsympathetic, regarded this earth with envious eyes, and slowly and surely drew their plans against us.
(Book 1, Ch. 1, p. 7)

The influence of Darwin's ideas can also be seen in the detailed physical description of the Martians in Book 2, Chapter 2.

Furthermore, they have also evolved into telepaths.

Key quotation

I am convinced — as firmly as I am convinced of anything — that the Martians interchanged thoughts without any physical intermediation.
(Book 2, Ch. 2, p. 129)

However, by the end of the novel, as a result of the Martian invasion, the human race is also evolving, not physically but in terms of both technology and morality and a 'commonweal of mankind' (Book 2, Ch. 10, p. 179) is beginning to develop. Wells explicitly refers to this much improved humanity when he has his narrator comment on the opening page: 'It is curious to recall some of the mental habits of those departed days' (p. 7).

Key quotation

The intellectual side of man already admits that life is an incessant struggle for existence…
(Book 1, Ch. 1, p. 8)

Key quotation

They have become practically mere brains, wearing different bodies according to their needs just as men wear suits of clothes and take a bicycle in a hurry or an umbrella in the wet.
(p. 129)

GRADE *FOCUS*

How will you be assessed on theme-based questions?

Grade 8

Students need to 'sustain a convincing, informed personal response to explicit and implicit meanings of texts'.

Grade 5

Students should 'develop a generally coherent and engaged response to explicit and implicit meanings of texts'. Even at the lower level of Grade 5, you need to do far more than merely identify themes. You should explain what techniques Wells uses to present these themes within the novel and what impact this presentation of theme will have on readers. For example, in what ways does Wells present colonisation and how might this make his contemporary readers feel about the British Empire?

REVIEW YOUR LEARNING

(Answers are given on p. 102.)

1 Which six themes have been identified in this section of the guide?

2 What does the novel suggest about the nature of humanity?

3 What can we learn about the British Empire from Wells's treatment of the theme of imperialism?

4 How does the artilleryman's criticism of the stifling nature of Victorian society relate to Wells's own early personal experience?

5 Which characters are most identified with the theme of evolution?

6 Why does Wells's attitude to war seem ambivalent?

7 Why does the narrator appear to have some sympathy with the behaviour of the Martians?

Target your thinking

- What features does the term 'style' refer to? (**AO2**)
- What is characteristic about Wells's style? (**AO2**)
- How does Wells create suspense? (**AO2**)
- In what ways does Wells use language for effect? (**AO2**)

A definition of style

A novelist's style is his or her distinctive manner of writing, i.e. what makes his or her writing unique. When responding to any examination question on *The War of the Worlds*, a relevant analysis of Wells's style will definitely boost your grade.

Narrative structure

Although this is obviously a work of fiction, Wells deliberately tries to create the impression that his narrator is writing a historical text — as, indeed, the title suggests. Consequently, he frequently refers to supposedly valid primary historical sources, generally a first person eye-witness account, but sometimes it is a real-life newspaper or a real-life academic, e.g. his reference to 'that distinguished anatomist, Professor Howes' (Book 2, Ch. 2, p. 125). Other references are to fictional academics, such as the acknowledgement that 'Carver's suggestions as to the reason of the rapid death of the Martians is so probable as to be regarded almost as a proven conclusion' (Book 2, Ch. 10, p. 177).

At other times the narrator does not refer to a specific source, and so takes on a more panoramic and omniscient narrative perspective, for example, when he writes so knowledgeably about geographical and climatic conditions upon Mars in the opening chapter. A careful reader may wonder how a first person narrator living at that time could possibly know all of this. Certainly, Ogilvy's observatory, which is also described in the opening chapter, does not seem to possess a telescope powerful enough to provide this kind of familiar detail. However, Wells is able to pull off the deceit partly owing to the fact that his narrator is addressing us from the future and so is invested with hindsight and the research he has done since the invasion.

Another clever narrative device is Wells's use of the **vicarious** accounts of Ogilvy, the artilleryman and his younger brother in order to overcome

vicarious: not experienced first-hand but second-hand, for example, conveyed through the account or senses of another person

the natural limitations of the first person viewpoint. If you re-read the first five chapters carefully, it is difficult to see when Ogilvy would have had an opportunity to inform the narrator in such precise detail about the cylinder he discovered in Book 1, Chapter 2 before his untimely death later on that day. Also, the narrator's knowledge of what these proxy narrators are thinking and feeling at the time of their experience is rather too detailed and, thus, more the province of a third person omniscient narrator:

> At once, with a quick mental leap, he linked the Thing with the flash upon Mars.
>
> (Book 1, Ch. 2, p. 15)

Wells furthers the illusion of the novel being a historical text through the narrator's occasional references to his own academic background:

> My particular province is speculative philosophy. My knowledge of comparative physiology is confined to a book or two...
>
> (Book 2, Ch. 10, p.177)

At another point in the novel he asserts that he has 'a certain claim to at least an elementary knowledge of psychology...' (Book 2, Ch. 2, p. 129). In the closing chapter, Wells also has the narrator suggest that the text that we are reading is actually part of an ongoing global academic study of the Martians.

For more on the narrative structure, see the sections on the narrator and his brother in the 'Characterisation' section of this guide.

Philosophical speculation

As is made clear above, Wells characterises his narrator as a speculative philosopher. In the nineteenth century, this would have been entirely compatible with writing a historical account, though much less acceptable today as such authorial intrusiveness could well be regarded as unacademic and a hindrance to the pursuit of historical accuracy. However, there was great precedent in Wells's time for such an approach to the writing of history and one particular influence on Wells in this respect is undoubtedly the greatest historian, essayist and philosopher of his day, Thomas Carlyle. (See the part entitled 'Carlyle and the politics of the Apocalypse' in the 'Context' section of this guide.)

This aspect of Wells's writing style is highly entertaining because of the frequently unusual and undoubtedly controversial nature of the ideas which he has such characters as the narrator, the artilleryman and the curate articulate. For example, in both the opening and concluding chapters of the novel, Wells has his narrator make many pronouncements on the nature of man.

However, the wildest and some of the most fascinating and speculative ideas are given to the artilleryman, a character that Wells deliberately

Build critical skills

Does Wells hide these 'breaches' of the first person narrative structure successfully or is this a weakness in the novel? What do you think?

Key quotation

I cannot but regret, now that I am concluding my story, how little I am able to contribute to the discussion of the many debatable questions which are still unsettled.
(Book 2, Ch. 10, p. 177)

Key quotation

Yet so vain is man, and so blinded by his vanity...
(Book 1, Ch. 1, p. 8)

distances himself from through the narrator's growing disillusionment with him. And yet, the artilleryman's notion of a largely compliant human race under the occupation of the brutal Martians, with a small but defiant underground resistance movement, is strikingly prophetic of events some forty-five years later in many parts of Europe which had the great misfortune to fall under the equally brutal occupation of Nazi Germany.

The artilleryman's dark vision is of a dystopia, that being an extremely unpleasant world. Wells distances himself from the idea because in his writing, he much prefers to search for a utopia, a much improved world — as is suggested at the end of this novel.

Scientific romance

One very obvious aspect of style is that Wells is writing science fiction, or 'scientific romance' as it was known at the end of the nineteenth century. Admittedly, in many respects, Wells is writing a novel of his time (as, for example, is indicated by the intensity with which he handles the key themes of Apocalypse and empire) but he is also writing a novel which is very much ahead of its time — and it is the dazzling brilliance of this vision which makes the novel such an intensely exciting read. Wells's predictions include:

- UFOs (the cylinders)
- extra-terrestrials (the Martians)
- space travel
- tanks (the tripods)
- flame throwers (the Heat-Rays)
- laser beams (the Heat-Rays)
- exoskeleton technology (the handling machines)
- chemical warfare (Black Smoke)
- total warfare: 'Never before in the history of warfare had destruction been so indiscriminate and universal' (Book 1, Ch. 11, p. 55).
- threat to the British Empire (First World War and Second World War)
- the rise of the United Nations (the 'commonweal of mankind')

Scientific jargon

quasi-science: pretend science

In tandem with the above, and again to enhance the illusion of authenticity and the consequent thrill ride of his science fiction classic, Wells makes frequent use of real scientific and sometimes **quasi-scientific** terminology:

- **Astronomy:** In Book 1, Chapter 1, Wells has his narrator use such astronomical and astronomically related terms as 'nebular hypothesis', 'secular cooling', 'the opposition of 1894' and 'spectroscope'.

- **Physics:** In Book 1, Chapter 6, in relation to the possible workings of the Heat-Ray, the narrator refers to: 'chamber of practically absolute non-conductivity', 'parallel beam' and 'parabolic mirror' (p. 28).
- **Biology:** In Book 2, Chapter 2, when describing the physiology of the Martians, the narrator uses such terms as 'pulmonary distress', 'complex apparatus of digestion' and 'gastric glands'.
- **Mechanics:** In Book 2, Chapter 3, when describing the handling-machine, the narrator uses such terms as 'oscillatory motion' and 'telescopic fashion'.

Quasi-science

Although Wells's use of quasi-science is a deliberate attempt to create tension and excitement by adding the illusion of 'realism' to the Martian invasion, it is also often lurid and sensationalist and there is a definite tongue-in-cheek aspect to it.

Key quotation

It is worthy of remark that a certain speculative writer of quasi-scientific repute, writing long before the Martian invasion, did forecast for man a final structure not unlike the actual Martian condition.
(Book 2, Ch. 2, p. 127)

In Book 2, Chapter 2 when Wells refers to 'a certain speculative writer of quasi-scientific repute', he is actually referring to himself and an article he had written in 1893 entitled *The Man of the Year Million* in which he proposed some very far-fetched ideas about how human beings might physically evolve. As he tells us in this chapter, his asexual Martians composed largely of brains and hands are modelled on the vision of a future human race proposed in that earlier work. The intentional sense of fun here is highlighted by his reference to that earlier text having been written in 'a foolish, facetious tone' (p. 127). Consequently, the second half of this chapter is a seemingly lighthearted parody of Darwin's *On the Origin of Species* (1859), the humour arising out of the extremely ludicrous and equally repulsive vision of the future humankind which, of course, Wells presents in the guise of the Martians.

However, there is also a much more serious intent here for, as the narrator also declares, 'There is many a true word written in jest...' (p. 127). As he goes on to explain, 'it is quite credible that the Martians may be descended from beings not unlike ourselves, by a gradual development of brain and hands...at the expense of the rest of the body' (p. 127). The key words which relate this 'facetious' vision of the future to Darwin's theory of evolution are 'descended', 'gradual' and 'development'.

metonymy: a figure of speech in which one aspect of a thing is used to represent the whole, e.g. 'hand' for human being

The moral here is one which is propounded throughout Victorian literature, for example in the essays of Thomas Carlyle and the novels of Charles Dickens, that being that as a result of the industrial revolution, the perception of humanity has been detrimentally transformed. Human beings are now quantified as units of production in a philosophy of rationalism and materialism, hence Wells's reduction of the Martians to no more than a brain (for rational thought) and hands (for manufacture). As in Dickens' *Hard Times*, 'hand' is most likely being used as a **metonymy**, thus suggesting that a person's perceived value lies only in what he/she can produce.

Key quotation

The brain alone remained a cardinal necessity. Only one other part of the body had a strong case for survival, and that was the hand…While the rest of the body dwindled, the hands would grow larger..
(Book 2, Ch. 2, p. 127)

Wells's language further parodies Darwin through the use of such phrases as 'cardinal necessity' and 'case for survival'. The damning point about this vision of a future human race, however, is that 'Without the body the brain would, of course, become a mere selfish intelligence, without any of the emotional substratum of the human being' (p. 127). The continuing pseudo-scientific register, which is maintained through the use of such quasi-scientific terms as 'emotional substratum', presents a misleadingly dispassionate analysis. In reality, Wells is not wildly speculating about some hypothetical future physical transformation of humanity, but expressing a profound concern about the moral degeneration of his own society.

Imagery

Another aspect of Wells's use of language is the number of imagery patterns which run throughout the book and which tend to work on a subliminal level, thus influencing the reader subconsciously…rather like the way in which advertising is often meant to work.

One of these is the apocalyptic imagery pattern which consists of references to such things as appear prominently in the Book of Revelation, e.g. fire, smoke, thunder and storms. The effect is to generate fear and excitement. (For more on this, see 'Millenarianism' in the 'Contexts' section of this guide and 'Apocalypse' in the 'Themes' section of this guide.)

A second prominent imagery pattern is the frequent comparison which takes place between humans and lower forms of life such as animals or insects. This reinforces the impression of Martian evolutionary supremacy and includes references such as:

They must have bolted as blindly as a flock of sheep.

(Book 1, Ch. 6, p. 30)

I could see the people who had been with me in the river scrambling out of the water through the reeds, like little frogs…

(Book 1, Ch. 12, p. 65)

Or did they interpret our spurts of fire, the sudden stinging of our shells, our steady investment of their encampment, as we should the furious unanimity of onslaught in a disturbed hive of bees?

(Book 1, Ch. 15, p. 86)

So, setting about it as methodically as men might smoke out a wasps' nest, the Martians spread this strange stifling vapour over the Londonward country.

(Book 1, Ch. 15, p. 90)

Description

Writing at a time when the cinema was barely a reality, and television was a good half-century away, Wells's audience would be well used to creating their own motion pictures within their minds providing a writer was skilful enough to use sufficiently vivid description and imagery. (The first commercial cinema was Vitascope Hall which opened on July 26, 1896, in New Orleans.)

Turn to almost any page of the novel and, if you read carefully enough, you will find Wells's intensely detailed 'word-paintings' filling your mind with immensely visual and, frequently, multi-sensory depictions of the scenes that he has firstly vividly experienced within his own imagination.

> The night was warm and still, and a little oppressive; the sound of guns continued intermittently, and after midnight there seemed to be sheet lightning in the south.
>
> (Book 1, Ch. 14, p. 80)

Build critical skills

Which three senses are appealed to in the quotation on the left?

Contrast

Contrast is when opposites are juxtaposed in order to create an interesting or exciting effect. When reading the passage from *The War of the Worlds* provided for you by your examination board, do look out for this as it is a major feature of Wells's style. Wells uses contrast both on a local level in the sense of there being a great dissimilarity between elements within a limited section of text, for example the contrast between the vibrant planet Earth and the dying planet Mars in the opening chapter. But he also uses contrast on a much larger scale, for example the contrast between the chapters which describe the peaceful rural setting around Woking prior to the Martian onslaught and the hell-like scenes of devastation which appear in the chapters that follow it.

Wells also uses contrast with regard to action. A perfect example of this is the notable difference in pace between the chapters describing the frantic mass exodus out of London and the markedly more static chapters in which the narrator and the curate are trapped in the house in Sheen.

Furthermore, there are some very stark thematic contrasts such as the varying treatments of the central theme of war which range from **jingoism** to horror and desolation. Compare Wells's narrator's excited description of the downing of the Martian tripod in Book 1, Chapter 12, with the same character's suicidal despair when faced with a decimated and lifeless London in Book 2, Chapter 8.

Finally, there is also a startling contrast regarding modes of transport. The locals travel on foot, on a bike, on a horse and cart, or, if one of the elite such as Lord Hilton, by train. The Martians, on the other hand, have spacecraft, a flying machine and 100-foot-tall metal tripods.

jingoism: an extreme form of patriotism accompanied by an aggressive and warlike attitude to other nations; strongly prevalent in British society when the novel was written

Key quotation

And this Thing I saw! How can I describe it? A monstrous tripod, higher than many houses, striding over the young pine-trees, and smashing them aside in its career; a walking engine of glittering metal, striding now across the heather...
(Book 1, Ch. 10, p. 46)

Action

Another very distinguishing characteristic of Wells's style is the focus on large-scale action. The main types of action tend to involve military engagements or people trying to flee from the Martians on foot, by train or by sea.

Key quotation

...the stream of flight rising swiftly to a torrent, lashing in a foaming tumult round the railway stations, banked up into a horrible struggle about the shipping in the Thames, and hurrying by every available channel northward and eastward.
(Book 1, Ch. 16, p. 92)

See the 'Plot and structure' section of this guide just to get some indication of the staggering number of events which take place in this novel!

Suspense

As Wells is writing an adventure story, the main focus of interest is on the plot rather than on the characters and, therefore, it is essential that he continually generate suspense. Consequently, Wells regularly includes minor details that arouse the reader's curiosity as to what happens next, e.g. the ashy clinker falling off the cylinder as the circular top rotates in Book 1, Chapter 2 and the 'faint stirring' from within the cylinder in Book 1, Chapter 3. Both details are indications of the Martians preparing to exit their craft and so launch their invasion.

Wells further excites his reader, and so creates an additional layer of suspense, with clever, unpredictable plot twists which have the effect of taking the reader totally by surprise:

- the sudden deaths of Ogilvy, Henderson and Stent in Book 1, Chapter 5, characters that the reader might reasonably have expected to feature far more prominently in the novel
- the unexpected destruction of the mighty Martian tripod in Book 1, Chapter 12
- and, ultimately, the deaths all of the Martians as a result of something so minute and primitive as bacteria (Book 2, Chapter 8)

Dramatic irony

Much of the suspense is also rooted in the clever use of Chapter 1 as a prologue in which Wells has the narrator provide the reader with information to which the characters are not privy, a use of **dramatic irony**. Tension arises out of the fact that we know that there are dangerous Martians hell-bent on world conquest inside the cylinders — but the hapless locals do not!

dramatic irony: when the reader or audience 'know more' than the characters are aware of

Shakespeare uses a similar device in *Romeo and Juliet*. Excitement arises out of the fact that although we might know what happens, we do not know how it will happen. And, furthermore, Wells (unlike Shakespeare) does not furnish us with the final conclusion in his prologue, but just enough to whet our appetites, and thus we are compelled to read on in order to find out how the story ultimately ends.

GRADE *FOCUS*

You are not likely to be asked a question in the examination that focuses only on style. However, in order to gain the highest grades, you will need to explain how aspects of style such as narrative tone, settings and imagery contribute to the presentation of character or theme.

REVIEW YOUR LEARNING

(Answers are given on p. 102.)

1 How would you define the term 'a writer's style'?
2 Which character does Wells use to extend the first person narrator's reach?
3 Which author does Wells appear to be modelling his style on when he has his narrator refer to himself as a 'speculative philosopher'?
4 Why does Wells use so much scientific jargon in the novel?
5 What does 'dramatic irony' mean?
6 In what way could the novel be regarded as an action novel?
7 What were Wells's main intentions when using so much quasi-scientific language in the novel?

Target your thinking

- What sorts of questions will you have to answer?
- What is the best way to plan your answer?
- How can you improve your grade?
- What do you have to do to achieve the highest grade?

Your response to a question on *The War of the Worlds* will be assessed in a 'closed book' English Literature examination, which means that you are not allowed to take copies of the examination text into the examination room. Different examination boards will test you in different ways and it is vital that you know on which paper the nineteenth-century novel will be so that you can be well-prepared on the day of the examination.

Whichever board you are studying, the following table explains which paper and section the novel appears in and gives you information about the sort of question you will face and how you will be assessed.

Marking

The marking of your responses varies according to the board your school or you have chosen. Each examination board will have a slightly different mark scheme, consisting of a ladder of levels. The marks you achieve in each part of the examination will be converted to your final overall grade. Grades are numbered from 1–9, with 9 being the highest.

It is important that you familiarise yourself with the relevant mark scheme(s) for your examination. After all, how can you do well unless you know exactly what is required?

Assessment Objectives for individual assessments are explained in the next section of the guide.

Approaching the examination question

First impressions

First read the whole question and make sure you understand exactly what the task requires you to do. It is very easy in the highly pressured atmosphere of the examination room to misread a question and this can be disastrous. Under no circumstances should you try to twist the

Examination board	Eduqas	OCR
Paper and section	Component 2 Section B	Paper 1 Section B
Type of question	Extract-based question requiring response to aspect of extract and response to the same or similar aspect in the novel as a whole.	Extract-based question requiring response to aspect of extract and response to the same or similar aspect in the novel as a whole. OR A question requiring the exploration of character, theme (or possibly stylistic aspect) in 'at least two moments from the novel'.
Closed book?	Yes	Yes
Choice of question?	No	Yes
Paper, section and lengths	Paper 2 = 2 hours 30 minutes Section B = 45 minutes	Paper 1= 2 hours Section B = 45 minutes
Percentage of whole grade	20% of Literature grade	25% of Literature grade
AOs assessed	AO1 AO2 AO3	AO1 AO2 AO3 AO4
Is AO4 (SPaG) assessed in this section?	No	Yes

question to the one that you have spent hours revising or the one that you did brilliantly on in your mock exam!

Are you being asked to think about how a character or theme is being presented or is it a description of a place? Make sure you know so that you will be able to sustain your focus later.

Look carefully at any bullet points you are given. They are there to help and guide you.

The two boards which offer *The War of the Worlds* as a text both use an extract-based question. However, the wordings and formats of the questions are slightly different.

SPaG: spelling, punctuation and grammar

Eduqas

A typical exam-style character question would be like this:

> You should use the extract below and your knowledge of the whole novel to answer this question.
>
> Write about turning points in the narrator's life as presented in the novel.
>
> In your response you should:
>
> - refer to the extract and the novel as a whole
> - show your understanding of characters and events in the novel
> - refer to the contexts of the novel
>
> (Extract taken from Book 2, Ch. 8, p. 167: 'London about me gazed at me spectrally…')

A typical exam-style thematic question would look like this:

> You should use the extract below and your knowledge of the whole novel to answer this question.
>
> Write about how the trauma caused by the Martian invasion is presented at different points in the novel.
>
> In your response you should:
>
> - refer to the extract and the novel as a whole
> - show your understanding of the characters and events
> - refer to the contexts of the novel
>
> (Extract taken from Book 1, Ch. 13, p. 70: 'Why are these things permitted?…')

OCR

A typical exam-style character question looks like this:

> Explore how Wells presents ideas about what makes a survivor through the presentation of the narrator's younger brother, in this extract and elsewhere in the novel.
>
> (Extract taken from Book 1, Ch. 16, p. 94: 'It was no time for pugilistic chivalry…')

A typical exam-style thematic question looks like this:

> 'The Martians' invasion is really a representation of human nature at its worst.' How far do you agree with this view?
>
> Explore at least two moments from the novel to support your ideas.

GRADE **BOOSTER**

Both boards assess AO1 and AO2 in this section of the paper. Always make sure you fully cover both of these AOs in your response, even if they do not seem to be signposted clearly in the question.

When responding to a question which is based on an extract, your next step is to *read the passage* very carefully, trying to get an overview or general impression of what is going on, and what or who is being described.

'Working' the text

Now read the passage again, underlining or highlighting any words or short phrases that you think might be related to the focus of the question and are of special interest. For example, they might be surprising, unusual or amusing. You might have a strong emotional or analytical reaction to them or you might think that they are particularly clever or noteworthy.

These words or phrases may work together to produce a particular effect, or to get you to think about a particular theme, or may encourage you to explore the methods the writer uses to present a character in a particular way for their own purposes. You may pick out examples of literary techniques such as lists or use of imagery, or sound effects such as alliteration or onomatopoeia. You may spot an unusual word order, sentence construction or use of punctuation. The important thing to remember is that when you start writing you must try to *explain the effects* created by these words and phrases or techniques, and not simply identify what they mean. Above all, ensure that you are answering the question.

Planning your answer

It is advisable to write a brief plan before you start writing your response to avoid repeating yourself or getting into a muddle. A plan is not a first draft. In fact, if your plan consists of full sentences at all, you are probably eating into the time you have available for writing a really insightful and considered answer.

However, a plan is important because it helps you to gather and organise your thoughts, but it should consist of brief words and phrases.

You may find it helpful to use a diagram of some sort — perhaps a spider diagram or flow chart. This may help you to keep your mind open to new ideas as you plan so that you can slot them in. You could make a list instead. The important thing is to choose a method that works for you.

If you have made a spider diagram, arranging your thoughts is a simple matter of numbering the branches in the best possible order.

The other advantage of having a plan is that if you run out of time, the examiner can look at the plan and may be able to give you an extra mark or two based on what you were about to do next.

Writing your answer

Now you are ready to start writing your answer. The first thing to remember is that you are working against the clock and so it's really important to use your time wisely.

It is possible that you may not have time to deal with all of the points you wish to make in your response. If you simply identify several language features and make a brief comment on each, you will be working at a fairly low level. The idea is to select the ones that you find most interesting and develop them in a sustained and detailed manner. In order to move up the levels in the mark scheme, it is important to write a lot about a little, rather than a little about a lot.

You must also remember to address the whole question as you will be penalised if you fail to do so.

If you have any time left at the end of the examination, do not waste it! Check carefully that your meaning is clear and that you have done the very best that you can. Look back at your plan and check that you have included all your best points. Is there anything else you can add? Keep thinking until you are told to put your pen down.

Referring to the author and title

You can refer to Wells either by name (make sure you spell it correctly) or as 'the writer'. You should never use his first name (Herbert) — this sounds as if you know him personally. You can also save time by giving the novel title in full the first time you refer to it, and afterwards simply referring to it as 'the novel'.

GRADE BOOSTER

Do not lose sight of the author in your essay. Remember that the novel is a construct — the characters, their thoughts, their words, their actions have all been created by Wells — so most of your points need to be about what Wells might have been trying to achieve. In explaining how his message is conveyed to you, for instance through an event, something about a character, use of symbolism, personification, irony and so on, don't forget to mention his name.

For example:

- Wells makes it clear that…

- It is evident from…that Wells is inviting the reader to consider…

- Here, the reader may well feel that Wells is suggesting…

Writing in an appropriate style

Remember that you are expected to write in a suitable register. This means that you need to use an appropriate style. This means:

- *not* using colloquial language or slang, e.g. 'The Martians are nasty pieces of work. Toe-rags really.' (The only exception is when quoting from the text.)

- *not* becoming too personal, e.g. 'The narrator's cool, right, 'cos he…'
- using suitable phrases for an academic essay, e.g. 'It could be argued that', not 'I reckon that…'
- not being too dogmatic. Don't say 'This means that…' It is much better to say 'This suggests that…'

You are also expected to be able to use a range of technical terms correctly. However, if you can't remember the correct name for a technique but can still describe it, and explain the effect it creates, you should still go ahead and do so.

The first person ('I')

It is perfectly appropriate to say 'I feel' or 'I think'. You are being asked for your opinion. Just remember that you are being asked for your opinion about *what* Wells may have been trying to convey in his novel (his themes and ideas) and *how* he does this (through characters, events, language, form and structure of the novel).

Spelling, punctuation and grammar (AO4)

Although your spelling, punctuation and grammar are only assessed by OCR on the nineteenth-century novel, you cannot afford to forget that you will demonstrate your grasp of the novel through the way you write, so take great care with this and don't be sloppy. If the examiner cannot understand what you are trying to say, he or she will not be able to give you credit for it.

How to raise your grade

The most important advice is to answer the question which is in front of you, and you need to start doing this straight away. When writing essays in other subjects, you may have been taught to write a lengthy, elegant introduction explaining what you are about to do. You have only a short time in the Literature examination so it's best to get cracking as soon as you've gathered your thoughts together and made a brief plan.

Sometimes students go into panic mode because they don't know how to start. It is absolutely fine to begin your response with the words, 'In this extract Wells presents…'

Begin by picking out interesting words and phrases and unpicking or exploring them within the context or focus of the question. For example, if the question is about the way that fear is presented, you need to focus on picking out words and phrases to do with fear.

What methods has the writer used? Although there are a whole range of methods with which you need to be familiar, it might be something as simple as a powerful adjective. What do you think is the impact of

GRADE *BOOSTER*

If you can't decide whether a phrase is a simile or a metaphor, it helps to just refer to it as an image.

GRADE *BOOSTER*

It is important to make the individual quotations you select brief and to try to *embed* them. This will save you time, enabling you to develop your points at greater depth and so raise your grade.

that word? It might be that the word you are referring to has more than one meaning. If that's the case, the examiner will be impressed if you can discuss what the word means to you, but can also suggest other meanings. Is context relevant here? In other words, would Wells's readers view fear differently at a time when there was growing international tension? What might Wells have been trying to express about fear when he chose this word or phrase?

It is likely that you will find it easier to address AO2 (methods) when writing about the extract as you have the actual words to hand.

Is there an actual overall effect? For instance, you may have noticed Wells's frequent use of lists of adjectives which create intensely vivid impressions, so as well as analysing individual words in the list (not necessarily all of them — just the most interesting ones) you could also describe the cumulative effect. An examiner would be particularly impressed if you were able to spot the cumulative effect of a semantic field, i.e. a group of words within a text which all relate to the same subject or idea.

Be very careful about lapsing into narrative. If you are asked about how Wells presents the narrator, remember that the focus of the question is about the methods that Wells uses. Do not simply tell the examiner what the narrator does or what he is like; this is a very common mistake.

Remember you also have to deal with the focus of the question in 'the novel as a whole' in the case of Eduqas and, for OCR, 'elsewhere in the novel' or in 'at least two moments from the novel'. You will be penalised if you do not do this so you *must* leave time. If you feel you have more to offer in terms of comments on the extract, leave a space so that you can return to it if necessary.

Key points to remember

- Do not just jump straight in. Spending time wisely in those first moments may gain you extra marks later.

- Write a brief plan.

- Remember to answer the question.

- Refer closely to *details* in the passage in your answer, support your comments, and remember you must also refer to other parts of the novel.

- Use your time wisely. Try to leave a few minutes to look back over your work and check your spelling, punctuation and grammar, so that your meaning is clear and so that you know that have done the very best that you can.

- Keep an eye on the clock!

GRADE *FOCUS*

Grade 5

Students will have a clear focus on the text and the task and will be able to 'read between the lines'. They will develop a clear understanding of the ways in which writers use language, form and structure to create effects for the readers. They will use a range of detailed textual evidence to support comments. They will show understanding of the idea that both writers and readers may be influenced by where, when and why a text is produced.

Grade 8

Students will produce a consistently convincing, informed response to a range of meanings and ideas within the text. They will use ideas that are well-linked and will often build on one another. They will dig deep into the text, examining, exploring and evaluating the writer's use of language, form and structure. They will carefully select finely judged textual references that are well integrated in order to support and develop their response to the text. They will show perceptive understanding of how contexts shape texts and responses to texts.

Aiming for a Grade 9

To reach the very highest level you need to have thought about the novel more deeply and produce a response which is conceptualised, critical and exploratory at a deeper level. You might, for instance, challenge accepted critical views in evaluating whether the writer has always been successful. If, for example, you think Wells set out to create loathing for the Martians, how successful do you think he has been?

You need to make original points clearly and succinctly and convince the examiner that your viewpoint is really your own, and a valid one, with constant and careful reference to the text. This will be aided by the use of short and apposite (meaning really relevant) quotations, skilfully embedded in your answer along the way (see 'Sample essays').

REVIEW YOUR LEARNING

(Answers are given on p. 103.)

1 Can you take your copy of the novel into the exam?

2 Why is it important to read the whole question carefully before you do anything else?

3 Why is it important to plan your answer?

4 Why is it important to keep an eye on the clock?

5 Will you be assessed on spelling, punctuation and grammar in your response to *The War of the Worlds*?

6 What should you do if you finish ahead of time?

All GCSE examinations are pinned to specific areas of learning that the examiners want to be sure the candidates have mastered. These are known as Assessment Objectives or AOs. If you are studying *The War of the Worlds* as an examination text for Eduqas or OCR, the examiner marking your examination response will be trying to give you marks, using the particular mark scheme for that board. However, all mark schemes are based on fulfilling the key AOs for English Literature.

Assessment Objectives

The Assessment Objectives that apply to your response to *The War of the Worlds* are as follows.

For Eduqas and OCR:

AO1	Read, understand and respond to texts. Students should be able to:
	• maintain a critical style and develop an informed personal response
	• use textual references, including quotations, to support and illustrate interpretations.
AO2	Analyse the language, form and structure used by a writer to create meanings and effects, using relevant subject terminology where appropriate.
AO3	Show understanding of the relationship between texts and the contexts in which they were written.

For OCR only:

AO4	Use a range of vocabulary and sentence structures for clarity, purpose and effect, with accurate spelling and punctuation.

You can't forget about AO4 entirely even if it is not applicable to your examination board for this text as it will probably be assessed on another part of the paper, usually Section A. That being said, if your spelling or punctuation leaves something to be desired at least you can lift your spirits by reminding yourself that AO4 is only worth about 5% of your total mark.

What skills do you need to show?

Let's break the Assessment Objectives down to see what they really mean.

AO1

> **AO1** Read, understand and respond to texts. Students should be able to:
> - maintain a critical style and develop an informed personal response
> - use textual references, including quotations, to support and illustrate interpretations.

At its most basic level, this AO is about having a good grasp of what a text is about and being able to express an opinion about it within the context of the question. For example, if you were to say, 'The novel is about a brutal Martian invasion' you would be beginning to address AO1 because you have made a personal response. An 'informed' response refers to the basis on which you make that judgement. In other words, you need to show that you know the novel well enough to answer the question.

It is closely linked to the idea that you are also required to **'use textual references including quotations to support and illustrate interpretations'**. This means giving short direct quotations from the text. For example, if you wanted to support the idea that the Martians are predatory, you could use a direct quote: '...blood obtained from a still living animal, in most cases from a human being, was run directly by means of a little pipette into the recipient canal...' (Book 2, Ch. 2, p. 125). Alternatively, you can simply refer to details in the text in order to support your views. So you might say, 'One of the most predatory and disturbing aspects of the Martian exploitation of human beings is that they siphon off and then infuse the blood of their human victims directly into their own veins.'

Generally speaking, most candidates find AO1 relatively easy. Usually, it is tackled well — if you answer the question you are asked, this Assessment Objective will probably take care of itself.

AO2

> **AO2** Analyse the language, form and structure used by a writer to create meanings and effects, using relevant subject terminology where appropriate.

AO2, however, is a different matter. Most examiners would probably agree that covering AO2 is a weakness for many candidates, particularly those students who only ever talk about the characters as if they were real people.

In simple terms, AO2 refers to the writer's methods and is often signposted in questions by the word 'how' or the phrase 'how does the writer present...?'

Overall AO2 is equal in importance to AO1 so it is vital that you are fully aware of this objective. The word **'language'** refers to Wells's use of words. Remember that writers choose words very carefully in order to achieve particular effects. They may spend quite a long time deciding between two or three words that are similar in meaning in order to create the precise effect that they are looking for.

If you are addressing AO2 in your response to *The War of the Worlds*, you will typically find yourself using Wells's name and exploring the choices he has made. For example, stating that in the novel's opening sentence Wells deliberately has the narrator assert that humanity was unknowingly being 'scrutinised and studied' by the Martians will set you on the right path to explaining why these words are an interesting choice.

You might say that the words suggest the powerlessness and vulnerability of an unsuspecting human race. Furthermore, they suggest the general superiority of the Martians by reducing humans to a lower level of species, that being one that is being studied as opposed the one that does the studying.

Language encompasses a wide range of writer's methods, such as the use of different types of imagery, words which create sound effects, irony and so on.

AO2 also refers to your use of **'subject terminology'**. This means that you should be able to use terms such as 'metaphor', 'alliteration' and 'hyperbole' with confidence and understanding. However, if you can't remember the term, don't despair — you will still gain marks for explaining the effects being created.

The terms **'form'** and **'structure'** refer to the kind of text you are studying and how it has been 'put together' by the writer. This might include the narrative technique being used — in *The War of the Worlds* Wells uses the first person narrator; the genre(s) the text is part of; the order of events and the effects created by it; and the way key events are juxtaposed. For example, Wells creates considerable dramatic power through the contrast between the depiction of the dormant cylinder in Chapter 3, which the narrator feels the need to protect from the stone-throwing boys, and the unexpected and sudden lethal destruction of the peaceful Deputation in Chapter 5. Effects of structure can also be seen in the writer's use of sentence lengths and word order (syntax).

Remember: if you do not address AO2 at all, it will be very difficult to achieve much higher than Grade 1, since you will not be answering the question.

AO3

> **AO3** Show understanding of the relationship between texts and the contexts in which they were written.

This AO, although not perhaps considered as important as AO1 and AO2, is still worth between 15% and 20% of your total mark in the examination as a whole, and so should not be underestimated.

To cover AO3 you must show that you understand the links between a text and when, why and for whom it was written. For example, some awareness of the often brutal and exploitative nature of the British Empire during the nineteenth century may well assist you to understand Wells's intentions in writing *The War of the Worlds* as a method of changing the attitudes of a largely middle-class readership towards British imperialism. Equally, some knowledge of Wells's background might give you a useful insight as to why he has the curate describe the Martian invasion as a punishment from God, owing to the extreme social inequality in Victorian society.

However, it is important to understand that context should not be 'bolted on' to your response for no good reason; you are writing about literature not history!

AO4

> **AO4** Use a range of vocabulary and sentence structures for clarity, purpose and effect, with accurate spelling and punctuation.

This AO is fairly self- explanatory and it is worth remembering that it is only assessed in your response to *The War of the Worlds* by OCR. However, a clear and well-written response should always be your aim. If your spelling is so bad or your grammar and lack of punctuation so confusing that the examiner cannot understand what you are trying to express, this will obviously adversely affect your mark.

Similarly, although there are no marks awarded for good handwriting, and none taken away for untidiness or crossing out, it is obviously important for the examiner to be able to read what you have written. If you believe your handwriting is so illegible that it may cause difficulties for the examiner, you need to speak to your school's examination officer in plenty of time before the exam. They may be able to arrange for you to have a scribe or to sit your examination using a computer.

Common mistakes

- **Retelling the story.** You can be sure that the examiner marking your response knows the story inside out. A key feature of the lowest grades is 'retelling the story'. Don't do it.

- **Quoting long passages.** Remember, the point is that every reference and quotation must serve the very specific point you are making. If you quote at length, the examiner will have to guess which bit of the quotation you mean to serve your point. Don't impose work on the examiner — be explicit about exactly which words you have found specific meaning in. Keep quotes short and smart.

- **Merely identifying literary devices.** You will never gain marks simply for identifying literary devices such as a simile or a metaphor. However, you can gain marks by identifying these features, exploring the reasons why you think the author has used them and offering a thoughtful consideration of how they might impact on readers, as well as an evaluation of how effective you think they are.

- **Giving unsubstantiated opinions.** The examiner will be keen to give you marks for your opinions, but only if they are supported by reasoned argument and evidence in the form of references to the text.

- **Writing about characters as if they are real people.** It is important to remember that characters are constructs — the writer is responsible for what the characters do and say. Don't ignore the author!

REVIEW YOUR LEARNING

(Answers are given on p. 103.)

1. What does AO1 assess?
2. What does AO2 assess?
3. What does AO3 assess?
4. What does AO4 assess?
5. Which two of the Assessment Objectives are the most important?
6. What should you avoid doing in your responses?

Below, you will find a Grade 8 response and a Grade 5 response to both an extract-based character question and an extract-based thematic question. All four responses have been fully annotated with examiners' comments so that you can see how the grades awarded relate to the four Assessment Objectives for GCSE English Literature. In other words, you will be able to see exactly how to write a top grade answer, and you will gain an insight into exactly what examiners are looking for when they award one of the above grades.

Question 1: Eduqas-style character-based

You are advised to spend about 45 minutes on this question. You should use the extract below and your knowledge of the whole novel to answer this question.

Write about the relationship between the narrator and the curate and how it is presented at different points in the novel. In your response you should:

- refer to the extract and the novel as a whole
- show your understanding of characters and events in the novel
- refer to the contexts of the novel

'All the work — all the Sunday-schools — What have we done — what has Weybridge done? Everything gone — everything destroyed. The church! We rebuilt it only three years ago. Gone! — swept out of existence! Why?'

Another pause, and he broke out again like one demented.

'The smoke of her burning goeth up for ever and ever!' he shouted.

His eyes flamed, and he pointed a lean finger in the direction of Weybridge.

By this time I was beginning to take his measure. The tremendous tragedy in which he had been involved — it was evident he was a fugitive from Weybridge — had driven him to the very verge of his reason.

'Are we far from Sunbury?' I said, in a matter-of-fact tone.

'What are we to do?' he asked. 'Are these creatures everywhere? Has the earth been given over to them?'

'Are we far from Sunbury?'

'Only this morning I officiated at early celebration —'

'Things have changed,' I said, quietly. 'You must keep your head. There is still hope.'

'Hope!'

'Yes. Plentiful hope — for all this destruction!'

I began to explain my view of our position. He listened at first, but as I went on the dawning interest in his eyes gave place to their former stare, and his regard wandered from me.

'This must be the beginning of the end,' he said, interrupting me. 'The end! The great and terrible day of the Lord! When men shall call upon the mountains and the rocks to fall upon them and hide them — hide them from the face of Him that sitteth upon the throne!'

I began to understand the position. I ceased my laboured reasoning, struggled to my feet, and, standing over him, laid my hand on his shoulder.

'Be a man!' said I. 'You are scared out of your wits! What good is religion if it collapses under calamity? Think of what earthquakes and floods, wars and volcanoes, have done before to men! Did you think God had exempted Weybridge? He is not an insurance agent, man.'

(Extract taken from Book 1, Ch. 13, pp. 70–71 of the Penguin Classics edition)

Student A, who is working at Grade 5, begins like this:

At the beginning of the passage it is clear that the curate thinks that God has let him down:

'All the work — all the Sunday-schools — What have we done — what has Weybridge done? Everything gone — everything destroyed. The church! We rebuilt it only three years ago. Gone!'

The curate is in despair because all of his hard work has been destroyed. Religion was very

1 An immediate concern here is that the student is writing about the curate as if he is a real person and not a literary creation fashioned by Wells in order to achieve particular effects.

2 This is an overly long quotation. Such excessive copying from the passage is a waste of the candidate's time.

important in this period and he certainly seems to have tried to do God's work! ←

The narrator, on the other hand, seems much calmer as shown when he says:

'Things have changed,' I said quietly.

The use of the word 'quietly' is very effective in creating this impression. Also, the way in which the narrator tries to reassure the curate by putting his hand on his shoulder also shows a caring and calm nature. In this respect he seems to be the stronger person. It is obvious that Wells admires the narrator and does not think too highly of the curate. Perhaps Wells is using the curate to attack religious hypocrisy.

One important idea that does come out in this passage is the narrator's contempt for the curate: 'You are scared out of your wits!' Personally, I think that the curate has every reason to be scared out of his wits as the Martians have just landed! However, by what the narrator says, Wells is suggesting that the curate is a coward. The narrator is clearly beginning to dislike the curate, even at this early stage in the novel. ←

4 This is a perceptive point about the use of language but the candidate has still not acknowledged that the author of this language is Wells, not the narrator.

5 Good point, but the candidate has not considered any deeper motives which might be underlying the narrator's reaction, e.g. his disgust at the 'unmanly' way in which the curate is acting and thus a consequent desire to calm him down.

7 The candidate has finally foregrounded the author and even provided a relevant comment regarding the historical background to the novel. Unfortunately, the valid reference to the curate's hypocrisy has not been developed.

3 The candidate's comment on the quotation provides a valid insight into the curate's personality but there are missed opportunities here for analysis of Wells's use of language, e.g. the use of fragments and heavy punctuation in order to suggest disjointed thinking owing to the despair which the candidate has correctly identified.

6 An additional concern is that the candidate has not yet begun to analyse the nature of the relationship between the two men and, instead, is showing every sign of simply writing two separate character studies.

8 This is a much better length quotation and certainly does prove the candidate's point.

9 The examination question has finally been directly addressed!

Student B, who is a Grade 8 candidate, starts like this:

One of the key factors in any relationship is the balance of power. A relationship may be founded on equality, but frequently one of the parties is more dominant than the other. In this relationship, Wells has clearly determined that the dominant character will be the narrator although, as we see in later parts of the novel, the curate does make a determined challenge for control.

1 Excellent. The candidate immediately begins to answer the set question.

2 Excellent again. The candidate is demonstrating a clear appreciation of the characters as literary constructs.

Because of the first person narrative structure of the novel, the narrator is frequently presented as an analytical observer which creates the impression of him being a calm and self-controlled individual. His thoughts are generally expressed in the narrative voice which consists of fluent, well-constructed sentences and which is supposedly being written from six years in the future whilst in the safe and comfortable environment of the study within his own house. Thus, there is no real need for him to sound anxious or distressed. The curate's voice, on the other hand, only exists within the calamity of the Martian invasion and is generally excitable. Through this contrast in language, Wells is again clearly portraying the narrator as the dominant party.

Wells immediately establishes the curate's weakness of character, and hence subordinate role in the relationship, through the despair which he has the curate express regarding the Martian destruction of everything that mattered to him. The short sentence structures and the frequent use of exclamation marks and dashes add to this effect. The rhetorical questions indicate that this is a man who is lost in confusion and doubt. His paraphrasing of biblical apocalyptic imagery further adds to creating the effect of a hysterical individual: 'The smoke of her burning goeth up for ever and ever!' This would be particularly powerful to Wells's contemporaries because a new millennium was about to dawn and many fundamentalist Christians were concerned that this could herald the end of the world.

Wells also uses the narrator's vantage point as story teller further to undermine the curate by including such speech tags as 'broke

3 This shows a most sophisticated appreciation of how the narrative structure can affect the characterisation.

4 A quotation could have been included here but the point is extremely well made and the candidate has saved time by not laboriously copying out a long sentence from the passage.

5 The candidate shows an admirable tenacity with regard to relating the point being made to the essay question.

6 Three powerful points about Wells's use of language are fired out here in three successive sentences. This is most perceptive and economical writing.

7 The candidate displays an excellent understanding of a pressing theological concern of that time.

out again like one demented' and 'shouted'. The narrator's own speech tags, however, are very self-flattering, e.g. 'I said, in a matter-of-fact tone'. Again, Wells is purposefully using language to undermine the reader's respect for the curate and to assert the narrator's general superiority.

8 Another most astute analysis of Wells's use of language and, again, an excellent use of a short, pertinent quotation as evidence in order to consolidate the point.

Wells also uses the narrator's actions and spoken words in order to indicate his authority. The narrator is presented as the one with the power to reassure and guide by the touch of a hand on the curate's shoulder. The admonition 'Be a man!' suggests the relationship between the two men is unequal and likely to be that of adult and child.

9 Another extremely perceptive point and, once more, a most rigorous focus upon the essay question has been maintained.

Student A continues as follows:

Because the curate has lost his belief in God he seems also to have lost his way in life and so is happy to follow the narrator. This is pretty much the pattern for the rest of the book. When the narrator decides to head towards Sheen the curate simply follows him. The narrator is obviously the leader out of the two men. Thus it is he who decides that they will leave the house at Halliford once the Black Smoke has been steamed away and travel to Sheen.

1 Some understanding of character.

2 At this point, the examiner might be wondering if the candidate has lost sight of the author again.

3 The candidate has clearly revised and appears to have sound knowledge of the sequence of events in the novel.

However, the narrator does not want to be responsible for the curate and does say that he wishes that the curate had stayed behind: 'I resolved to leave him — would that I had!' Wells is using dramatic foreshadowing here. The use of the exclamation mark adds to the suspense and makes the reader wonder why the narrator wishes so strongly that the curate had not gone with him.

4 Quotation from Book 2, Ch. 1, p. 116.

5 Clear understanding of effect, i.e. the comment about the exclamation mark.

In the house in Sheen, the relationship between the two men really begins to

6 The candidate now seems much more focused on the examination question and appears to be resisting the fatal temptation of simply summarising the story.

7 At this point, a stronger candidate might have suggested that the curate's inability to provide the dehydrated narrator with water is symbolic of the curate's crisis of faith.

11 The candidate ends with an appropriate quotation and an observation about Wells's use of this subplot as part of his overall structuring of the novel.

disintegrate. The narrator and the curate are trapped in the ruined house as a result of the fifth cylinder crash landing next to it. The narrator is knocked unconscious but when he comes round he finds the curate calmly trying to bring him round by dabbing water on him. The curate is doing this despite the fact that he is bleeding from a cut to his own head. This is similar to what happened when the narrator first met the curate who was watching over him after he had passed out from exhaustion and dehydration by the side of the river. Wells has created a pattern here, especially as water is mentioned in both sections. However, this calm behaviour does seem odd considering the curate's normal pattern of hysterical outbursts.

Unfortunately, the curate's calmness does not last long. It could that be the Wells does not want the reader to like the curate too much as eventually the narrator is going to kill him.

When the narrator does murder the curate with a meat-chopper, it does seem justified because the curate had been acting up by demanding food even though they are very short on supplies. Also, the curate was just about to give himself up to the Martians and the narrator was terrified of being caught and used as a blood bank.

Thus the relationship between the curate and the narrator is a tragic one which eventually ends in the death of the curate when the narrator reluctantly kills him. As the narrator stated much earlier in the novel: 'we had absolutely incompatible dispositions and habits of thought and action...' Wells has definitely used this one-sided relationship to create an interesting subplot to the main action of the Martian invasion.

8 A good linkage between related sections of the novel. Also, some analysis of the curate's character which, as the candidate suggests, does seem a little inconsistent at times.

9 Clear awareness of authorial intent, although it would have been even stronger if the candidate had phrased it as 'Wells is eventually going to have the narrator kill him.'

10 Quotation from Book 2, Ch. 3, p. 131.

Commentary on Student A's essay: Although the first half of the essay is weak, the second part is stronger and so allows the candidate to achieve a Grade 5. Overall, the essay is generally well-focused on the question and there has been a reasonably successful attempt to support the points being made via apt textual reference and some pertinent analysis. By the end of the essay, the candidate has demonstrated a clear enough understanding of the ways in which Wells uses language, form and structure. A little more could have been written regarding the relationship between the novel and the historical context.

AO4 (assessed by OCR only): The range and quality of sentence structures and vocabulary is always competent and, sometimes, quite sophisticated. Meaning is clearly conveyed and spelling, punctuation and grammar are very accurate.

Student B, working at Grade 8, continues in this way:

> However, by the time the two men become trapped inside the ruined house at Sheen, Wells's portrayal of the narrator becomes more one of a man who feels increasingly threatened by the curate. This is a most interesting shift in their dynamic and one which the reader could never have predicted. In fact, much of the excitement of the novel is derived from the continual twists and turns that Wells has deliberately written into the plot.
>
> Prior to arriving in Sheen, Wells does allow the curate to protest at a number of the narrator's decisions. For example, the curate tries to argue that they would be better staying put at the house in Halliford because it is 'safer'. However, the narrator's determination to be reunited with his wife makes him press on and, inevitably, the curate scuttles after him.
>
> The first indications of the power struggle which will ultimately result in the narrator murdering the curate occur early in Book 2 shortly after they have arrived at Sheen and begin observing the Martians through the peep hole in the wall. Wells has the narrator

1 A most insightful comment on a key aspect of Wells's style.

2 This candidate is always very keen to demonstrate awareness that the characters are literary devices and not real people.

85

inform the reader that the two men would 'strike each other, and thrust and kick' as they scrambled for this fascinating insight into the Martian base. Here, Wells intensifies the reader's impression of these tussles through the use of the rule of three violent verbs.

Wells may well be deliberately foreshadowing, and thus preparing the reader, for the greater violence to come though the narrator's description of these encounters. However, the sudden transformation of the two men into such viciousness over such a small matter does risk stretching the reader's credibility. It is also the case that a number of critics do question the realism of Wells's characterisation in this novel and, to be honest, the above scene could come over to the reader as a little farcical!

The struggle for dominance becomes more primal, and credible, when Wells shifts the focus of their conflict to food. The curate's unwillingness to ration and share equally the limited stock of sustenance available in the house could well justify the narrator's increasingly violent behaviour towards the curate because it is actually putting the narrator's life at risk. In Book 2, Chapter 4, 'The Death of the Curate', the narrator comments that 'There were times when I beat and kicked him madly...' Again, the reader might question the credibility of the characterisation as the violence now suddenly seems so one-sided whereas just before it was much more equally balanced.

However, if the war between the Martians and the human race can be seen as an evolutionary struggle for survival over limited natural resources between species on the large scale, then the struggle for

3 Quotation from Book 2, Ch. 3, p. 131.

4 Excellent analysis of the use of language in the memorised quotation and excellent use of subject terminology in referencing the use of the rule of three in relation to verbs.

5 Again, excellent use of subject vocabulary.

6 It certainly is refreshing, if a little unusual, to see such a high level of both confidence and critical awareness!

7 And again — this time pointing out more inconsistencies in Wells's characterisation.

food between the narrator and curate in this subplot could also be viewed as a dramatization of Darwin's theory of survival of the fittest on a much smaller, microcosmic scale.

Ultimately, the narrator's decision to strike the curate dead with a meat cleaver is credible, if somewhat shocking. The curate finally seems to have succumbed to the overwhelming guilt that he has been experiencing ever since the Martian invasion owing to his realisation that he has failed God by not condemning the social injustice and inequality which was rife in supposedly Christian Victorian society. Consequently, he has lost his sanity and is preparing to sacrifice himself, and hence the narrator, to the Martians.

There is one final closing stage in the relationship between the two men which takes place when the narrator, having escaped from the house in Sheen, stays overnight at the inn in Putney. During the one evening that he spends there, Wells has him reflect upon the killing of the curate. The narrator's final position on the matter is: 'I felt no condemnation...' Of course, whether or not such a judgment would be shared by a moralistic middle-class Victorian readership is another question, although the curate's self-proclaimed hypocrisy just prior to his death does align him with the 'Oppressors of the poor and needy' and, consequently, Wells has done his best to insure that the curate won't be missed!

8 This is a brilliant point and shows a most perceptive and subtle understanding of the relationship between Wells's narrative structure and the intellectual background of his day.

9 Again, the candidate shows an excellent awareness of the social and historical background to the novel here.

10 Quotation from Book 2, Ch. 7, p. 149.

11 Quotation from Book 2, Ch. 4, p. 137.

12 Another most appropriate reference to the historical context.

Commentary on Student B's essay: This is an extremely well-focused analysis which thoroughly addresses all of the Assessment Objectives and which explores how Wells uses a wide variety of literary devices in order to develop the relationship between the two characters. Most points made have been judiciously supported by most appropriate textual references. An excellent balance has been maintained between analysing the extract and exploring other key moments in the novel. The candidate takes every opportunity to make powerfully perceptive points regarding Wells's use of language, form and structure in order to create effects for the reader. All references to the historical context are very well integrated and extremely relevant in that they either explain how the historical circumstances of the time would have affected a contemporary reader's response to the novel or they explain how the historical background influenced Wells's writing of the novel.

AO4: (Assessed by OCR only) The range and quality of sentence structures and vocabulary is most sophisticated. Meaning is always conveyed with force and clarity. Paragraphing, spelling, punctuation and grammar are excellent.

The response does everything to achieve a Grade 8, and shows signs of going even higher.

Question 2: OCR-style theme-based

> You are advised to spend about 45 minutes on this question.
>
> 'In *The War of the Worlds*, Wells presents both the horror and the excitement of war.' How far do you agree with this view? Explore at least two moments from the novel to support your ideas.

Student X, who is working towards Grade 5, begins in this way:

H. G. Wells was a pacifist and his 1940 pamphlet, 'The Rights of Man', helped to create the United Nations and its idea of world peace. In fact, even in 1919 he was campaigning for world peace and wrote a book called 'The idea of a League of Nations'. The actual League of Nations was set up to try and prevent another world war but it failed because the Treaty of Versailles (1919) left many Germans, including Adolf Hitler, very angry and resentful. So, it is not surprising to find such anti-war ideas in his novel.

The first moment that I am going to explore for this theme occurs in Book 1, Chapter 12.

In this scene, the horror of war is clearly shown when Wells has the people in the

1 Some of the historical information is relevant but the candidate does seem to have momentarily lost sight of the fact that this is not a history examination!

2 The candidate seems more influenced by revised biographical notes about Wells's later passion for world peace than by the content of the novel or the ambivalence alluded to in the question.

4 The candidate has clearly closely revised a number of key 'moments' from the novel and so is able to make a valiant attempt at analysing the effects of Wells's use of language.

river scream as the Martian collapses. Wells increases this sense of horror when he describes the 'scaldingly hot' water. His use of language is multi-sensory and thus very effective.

Wells truly shows the horror of war when he uses such visceral phrases to describe the Martian's horrific injuries as 'tattered fragments of red flesh.' He also uses the word 'splashed' which gives the sense of lots of blood.

Other imagery that Wells uses in this scene is when he says: 'The decapitated colossus reeled like a drunken giant...' The simile really creates a powerful impression for the reader of the machine staggering around all over the place before it eventually collapses.

The violent language used in this scene shows the horror of warfare but also definitely helps to create excitement for the reader.

3 Good point, although technically, Wells is having his narrator describe the scene which is more indirect and removed than if he had actually written it as himself.

5 'Visceral' is an excellent choice of word and suggests that the candidate has far more potential than this essay shows.

6 A good analysis of the image, but not very relevant to the essay question. The candidate would have been better to have focused on the word 'decapitated' because it would be relevant to the candidate's argument that this 'moment' is really about the horrors of war.

7 The candidate seems to show only a superficial appreciation of the fact that the scene also presents war as being intensely exciting.

Student Y, who is working at Grade 8, starts like this:

One of the most exciting 'war' moments in the novel occurs in Book 1, Chapter 12, when Wells describes the intense battle between the British artillery and the Martians whilst the narrator and many other evacuees seek shelter in the River Thames. In this 'moment' Wells clearly presents both the horror and the excitement of war, something which he does throughout much of the novel. One way in which Wells communicates this sense of excitement is through use of the narrator's exclaimed outburst and the speech tag which describes it as 'something between a scream and a cheer'. The people around the narrator also experience the same sense of what Wells describes as 'exultation.'

The gory nature of war is graphically described, especially the description of the

1 The candidate is immediately focused upon the ways in which Wells reveals attitudes to war and quickly begins to analyse Wells's use of language.

89

Martian's head exploding inside the helmet of the tripod. However, Wells dehumanises the casualty by collectively describing the Martian and the tripod as 'the Thing'. Such dehumanisation of the enemy is an essential feature of any war propaganda and so, in the First World War, the British referred to the Germans as 'Huns'. Of course, in this particular instance, the enemy really is inhuman and, furthermore, the reader is unlikely to feel any compassion for the Martian, especially because of the indiscriminate killing of innocent humans which Wells has well established by this point in the novel, for example, the totally unprovoked attack on the peace Delegation at Horsell Common.

Wells also uses another tactic which is often found in propagandist war writing, that being associating your own forces with God: 'the Martian within the hood, was slain and splashed to the four winds of heaven…' The word splashed is particularly vivid and really does create a sense of the shocking and fatal injury inflicted upon the Martian, but the reference to the 'four winds of heaven' suggests that this was a totally justifiable act.

2 An excellent analysis of Wells's use of language and of use of language in general in connection with war writing.

3 The candidate clearly has an excellent knowledge of the novel.

4 Another excellent analysis of Wells's use of language.

Student X concludes as follows:

1 Although the candidate persists in a very one-sided view of the presentation of war within the novel, the essay remains highly relevant and the 'moment' is well chosen.

Wells's most frightening presentation of war is when the Martians invade London using the Black Smoke which appears to act just like poison gas. This section of the novel is told largely from the point of view of the narrator's brother, a technique that Wells uses in order to provide the reader with information that the first person narrator could not possibly know about. Through use of this evil chemical weapon which predicts the horrors of World War 1 the Martians

2 An excellent point about the narrative structure.

are able to destroy the artillery batteries which lie between them and London and create the mass panic which results in the exodus. As we see on the News every day war creates a refugee crisis and that also involves great misery such as sickness, poverty and hunger.

3 A quite perceptive and original point about one of the horrific consequences of warfare.

When describing the 'exodus', Wells uses the narrator's brother to show the masses of evacuees desperately seeking food and savagely battling with each other in desperation to escape. Wells refers to this at the beginning of Book 1, Chapter 16 as 'that swift liquefaction of the social body.' As Wells uses a lot of water imagery to describe the exodus from London caused by the Black Smoke, the 'liquefaction' image is very appropriate. It is as if society has simply dissolved and is now 'a roaring wave of fear', which is another quotation from the same section. This second quotation clearly suggests the idea of a mass movement of people and of them being in tremendous danger.

4 The candidate clearly knows the novel well and the analyses of the well-remembered quotations show clear understanding.

The word 'exodus' which appears in the title of Chapter 16 is a religious word which refers to Moses leading his people out of Egypt. It suggests that the Martian invasion is massive and that the humans are as defenceless to the Martians as the Israelites were to the Egyptians. As Victorian society was very religious, Wells's readers would have been very aware of what this image suggests about how vulnerable the humans really are. The main thing is that there is no sense of war being thrilling here, just horrifying and terrifying.

5 A relevant reference to the social and religious context in which the novel was written.

Commentary on Student X's essay: There is much to commend in this essay: the continual recognition of Wells as author, the candidate's knowledge of appropriate 'moments', some of the analyses of Wells's use of language, some of the contextual references, and the consistent manner in which the candidate has supported the interpretation of the presentation of war as being horrific through apt textual reference. The main issues, however, are that the interpretation is one-sided and the introduction was not sufficiently related to the question. However, there are enough positives to merit the award of Grade 5.

AO4 (assessed by OCR only): it is a well-written essay with very accurate SPaG and some excellent vocabulary.

Student Y concludes like this:

> Part of the narrator's, and possibly Wells's, excitement at the idea of war is as a result of a feeling of patriotic pride in the British armed forces. This is clear from a number of passages in the novel, including the one above. Such patriotism, or jingoism, was a result of rivalry with other European nations, especially Germany which also wanted its own global empire. But Wells also considers the other side of empire in his presentation of war, that being the brutal nature of wars of conquest.
>
> As Wells has his narrator tell us in Chapter 1, 'for countless centuries Mars has been the star of war…' Mars was actually the Roman God of War and, of course, the British ruling classes were given a classical education and so had both a knowledge and a great respect for Roman culture, even to the extent that the British Empire resembled it in many ways. Victorian public architecture was greatly influenced by classical design and Britain, like Rome, possessed a mighty empire which spanned the world. Therefore, when Wells depicts Martian colonisation as aggressive and exploitative, he may well also be symbolically characterising the British Empire as being the same.
>
> Certainly, when Wells has the narrator inform the reader of the extermination of

1 The candidate is referring to the previously analysed scene from Book 1, Chapter 12 in which the British artillery successfully destroy a Martian tripod.

2 This candidate *really* does know how to address the Assessment Objective relating to context.

3 An imaginative interpretation of Wells's possible use of symbolism. The most apt quotation has also been extremely well integrated.

the Tasmanians in the opening chapter, which he tactfully describes as being carried out by Europeans when, in fact, those Europeans were actually British colonists, he is making clear his disgust at wars of conquest. In the fictional world of the novel, however, the British forces are representing all of humanity, not narrow British self-interest, and they are fighting a defensive war, not a war of aggression. Thus, Wells's seemingly ambivalent attitude to war is, in fact, both moral and consistent.

There is also a sense in which the war with the Martians is welcomed by Wells in that it actually results in the destruction of the old way of life, including the British Empire, and in its place there is 'the conception of the commonweal of mankind'. Ultimately, what Wells seems to be advocating through his novel is not world war, but world peace.

4 The candidate remains extremely well focused upon the question, and the combination of historical reference and literary analysis is of a high order.

5 A strong conclusion which is extremely succinct and which adds a compelling overall summation of attitudes to war as presented in the novel. Furthermore, the candidate closes with a most stylish antithesis.

Commentary on Student Y's essay: This is an extremely well-focused analysis which thoroughly addresses all of the Assessment Objectives and which explores how Wells uses a wide array of literary devices in order to present two very contrasting attitudes towards war. All points made have been judiciously supported by most appropriate textual references and the candidate has clearly demonstrated an excellent understanding of characters and events in the novel. The candidate takes every opportunity to make powerfully perceptive points regarding Wells's use of language, style and structure in order to create effects for the reader. The references to the historical context have been well integrated and used in order to display a profound understanding of the novel.

AO4 (assessed by OCR only): the range and quality of sentence structures and vocabulary is most sophisticated. Meaning is always conveyed with force and clarity. Paragraphing, spelling, punctuation and grammar are excellent.

The response does everything to achieve at least a Grade 8.

Top ten quotations

Top ten characterisation quotations

The narrator

1 'Perhaps I am a man of exceptional moods...At times I suffer from the strangest sense of detachment from myself and the world about me...' (Book 1, Ch. 7, p. 32)

- Here, Wells tries to justify the frequently inconsistent manner of his narrator's behaviour as he so rapidly shifts between terror, curiosity and excitement with regard to the Martians.

2 'Be a man!' said I. 'You are scared out of your wits!' (Book 1, Ch. 13, p. 71)

- Both Wells and the narrator greatly admire manliness.

3 'In the silence of the night, with that sense of the nearness of God that sometimes comes into the stillness and the darkness, I stood my trial, my only trial, for that moment of wrath and fear.' (Book 2, Ch. 7, p. 149)

- A clear explanation of why the narrator kills the curate as well as an insight into his extremely rational nature which enables him to quickly clear his conscience of the act.

The narrator's brother

4 'I have set forth at length in the last chapter my brother's account of the road through Chipping Barnet...' (Book 1, Ch. 17, p. 104)

- The brother's main function is to act as a proxy narrator in order to provide credibility for the narrator's description of the exodus from London at which he was not present.

The curate

5 'Why are these things permitted? What sins have we done?' (Book 1, Ch. 13, p. 70)

- One of the defining qualities of the curate is his crisis of faith as a result of the invasion.

'There was poverty, sorrow; the poor were trodden in the dust, and I held my peace.' (Book 2, Ch. 4, p. 137)

6

- Wells appears to be using the curate to expose the religious hypocrisy of organised religion which preached Christianity but tolerated, even benefitted from, the misery of the poor.

The artilleryman

'Life is real again, and the useless and cumbersome and mischievous have to die. They ought to die.' (Book 2, Ch. 7, p. 157)

7

- The artilleryman obviously revels in the overthrow of the existing world order and his ruthlessness is also clearly revealed.

'I resolved to leave this strange undisciplined dreamer of great things to his drink and gluttony …' (Book 2, Ch. 7, p. 162)

8

- However, the artilleryman lacks the energy and motivation to do anything other than rail against society and fantasise about a heroic role for himself. At the same time, Wells distances himself from such subversive ideas.

The Martians

'The peculiar V-shaped mouth with its pointed upper lip, the absence of brow ridges, the absence of a chin beneath the wedge-like lower lip, the incessant quivering of this mouth, the Gorgon groups of tentacles…' (Book 1, Ch. 4, pp. 21–22)

9

- Wells's description of the invaders is deliberately designed to be as repulsive, grotesque and inhuman as possible and so differs markedly from other contemporary novels which had envisaged more man-like Martians.

'They seemed busy in their pit, and there was a sound of hammering and an almost continuous streamer of smoke.' (Book 1, Ch. 9, p. 40)

10

- This associates the Martians with two major influences on Victorian society, industrialisation and religion, namely the fear of the Apocalypse.

Top ten thematic quotations

Humanity

1 '...as men busied themselves about their various concerns they were scrutinized and studied, perhaps almost as narrowly as a man with a microscope might scrutinize the transient creatures that swarm and multiply in a drop of water.' (Book 1, Ch. 1, p. 7)

- Wells seems determined to attack the pompousness and arrogance of the British establishment of the day through such unflattering and belittling comparisons between the human race and the Martians.

2 'Yet so vain is man, and so blinded by his vanity...' (Book 1, Ch. 1, p. 8)

- Wells is frequently a severe critic of the human race, although sometimes his criticisms of human nature may really be aimed at the arrogant British establishment which controlled and personally benefited from the exploitative British Empire.

3 '...it has done much to promote the conception of the commonweal of mankind.' (Book 2, Ch. 10, p. 179)

- Much of Wells's writing expresses the hope of a morally improved humanity arising out of catastrophe.

Evolution

4 'The intellectual side of man already admits that life is an incessant struggle for existence, and it would seem that this too is the belief of the minds upon Mars.' (Book 1, Ch. 1, p. 8)

- Darwin's theory of evolution has massively influenced the novel in terms of both theme and plot.

5 '...we must remember what ruthless and utter destruction our own species has wrought, not only upon animals, such as vanished bison and the dodo, but upon its own inferior races.' (Book 1, Ch. 1, p. 9)

- The theme of Social Darwinism is also powerfully evident in the novel, that being that human beings, just like animals and plants, also compete in a struggle for survival in which the strongest inevitably overpower and destroy the weakest.

'We men, with our bicycles and road-skates, our Lilienthal soaring-machines, our guns and sticks and so forth, are just in the beginning of the evolution that the Martians have worked out.' (Book 2, Ch. 2, p. 129)

6

- Evolution is the driving force of life not just on Earth, but in the entire Universe.

War

'Something very like the war-fever that occasionally runs through a civilised community had got into my blood...' (Book 1, Ch. 10, p. 44)

7

- Wells sees war as inevitable and as an integral part of human nature.

'This isn't a war,' said the artilleryman. 'It never was a war, any more than there's war between men and ants.' (Book 2, Ch. 7, p. 152)

8

- A powerfully poetic statement on asymmetric warfare which beautifully encapsulates the military and technological superiority of the Martians and which ironically mirrors the military and technological superiority which the British Empire employed to bully and exploit less advanced societies around the world.

Empire

'...it has robbed us of that serene confidence in the future which is the most fruitful source of decadence...' (Book 2, Ch. 10, p. 179)

9

- The use of the word 'decadence' is a direct condemnation of the corrupting influence of Empire.

'Surely, if we have learnt nothing else, this war has taught us pity — pity for those witless souls that suffer our dominion.' (Book 2, Ch. 7, p. 149)

10

- Another outright attack on British imperialism.

Top ten moments

'Yet across the gulf of space, minds that are to our minds as ours are to those of the beasts that perish, intellects vast and cool and unsympathetic, regarded this earth with envious eyes, and slowly and surely drew their plans against us.' (Book 1, Ch. 1, p. 7)

1

- Just one of the many amazingly vivid and poetic statements in the opening chapter which generate enormous suspense.

2 'There were four or five boys sitting on the edge of the pit, with their feet dangling, and amusing themselves — until I stopped them — by throwing stones at the giant mass.' (Book 1, Ch. 3, p. 17)

- Wells shows the natural aggressiveness of humanity and simultaneously implants the subtle suggestion that the human race is still essentially primitive and Stone Age, especially when compared to the super-advanced Martians.

3 '…that swift liquefaction of the social body.' (Book 1, Ch. 16, p. 92)

- Throughout the novel, Wells continually paints a picture of the total destruction of the old world order as part of his apocalyptic vision of a new millennium which will take place with the dawn of the twentieth century.

4 'Before dawn the black vapour was pouring through the streets of Richmond, and the disintegrating organism of government was, with a last expiring effort, rousing the population of London to the necessity of flight.' (Book 1, Ch. 15, p. 91)

- Again, the Martian invasion tears down long established structures, ultimately making way for the new and much improved 'commonweal of man'.

5 'Never before in the history of warfare had destruction been so indiscriminate and so universal.' (Book 1, Ch. 11, p. 55)

- The Martian invasion is Wells's vision of the biblical Apocalypse but, also, is an amazing prophecy in its own right as it predicts the 'total war' of the First World War.

6 'Never before in the history of the world had such a mass of human beings moved and suffered together.' (Book 1, Ch. 17, p. 104)

- Movement, and the search for direction, both geographical and spiritual, is a major feature of the novel.

7 'For a time I believed that mankind had been swept out of existence, and that I stood there alone, the last man left alive.' (Book 2, Ch. 6, p. 147)

- Yet another amazingly poetic and suspenseful line. How many films have since been based on this incredibly dramatic and haunting idea?

'By the toll of a billion deaths man has bought his birthright of the earth, and it is his against all comers; it would still be his were the Martians ten times as mighty as they are.' (Book 2, Ch. 8, p. 168)

8

- Having one of the most basic organisms destroy the most evolutionary advanced of all, the Martians, is yet another of the powerful poetic ironies in the novel.

'Dim and wonderful is the vision I have conjured up in my mind of life spreading slowly from this little seed-bed of the solar system throughout the inanimate vastness of sidereal space.' (Book 2, Ch. 10, p. 179)

9

- In the concluding chapter, Wells conjures up yet another incredibly foresighted prediction, the human race colonising space!

'And strangest of all is it to hold my wife's hand again, and to think that I have counted her, and that she has counted me, among the dead.' (Book 2, Ch. 10, p. 180)

10

- In this closing sentence of the novel, Wells makes a very last-minute, and rather superficial, attempt to cater to the Victorian reader's love of romantic fiction. Compare this, for example, with the closing sentence of a genuine romance novel, Charles Dickens' *Great Expectations*: 'I took her hand in mine, and...I saw the shadow of no parting from her.'

- The Penguin Classic edition of *The War of the Worlds* (ISBN: 9780141441030). This contains a most useful biographical essay on Wells, a very helpful introduction to the novel and excellent explanatory notes which explain the meaning or significance of many of the references in the text. Furthermore, all page numbers in this guide relate to this edition of the novel.
- *Across the Zodiac* by Percy Greg, published by CreateSpace Independent Publishing Platform. ISBN: 9781511866910.
- Percival Lowell's 1895 book *Mars*, published by General Books LLC. ISBN: 9781151321145.
- George Chesney's *The Battle of Dorking* (1871), published by CreateSpace Independent Publishing Platform. ISBN: 9781494780562.

Useful websites

- www.gutenberg.org/ebooks/36 — the free Project Gutenberg e-book copy of *The War of the Worlds*. Using the search function on your browser, you can type in key words and quickly search for such things as particular passages or imagery patterns.
- www.shmoop.com/war-of-the-worlds-hg-wells/ — Shmoop. Extremely detailed (and most amusingly written) summaries of every chapter in the novel.
- http://en.wikipedia.org/wiki/The_War_of_the_Worlds — Wikipedia. Extremely detailed information about both the novel and the context.
- www.war-ofthe-worlds.co.uk/war_of_the_worlds.htm by John Gosling. A most useful and informative website dedicated to the novel and which is packed full of information about the background context, and consequent cultural impact, of Wells's novel.
- www.bbc.co.uk/news/magazine-15470903 — BBC. An interesting article about the 1938 radio dramatisation of *The War of the Worlds*.
- http://mars.nasa.gov/ — NASA. A fascinating and easy-to-read website which contains all sorts of interesting information about Mars, ranging from past historical misconceptions to the latest scientific discoveries.

Answers

Answers to the 'Review your learning' sections.

Context (p. 19)

1 1866–1946.

2 As a young man, he suffered serious ill-health as a result of malnutrition, and so having sufficient food to eat was a very important concern.

3 The heavy use of apocalyptic imagery and the regular sermonising on the flaws in human nature.

4 *Mars*.

5 The Martians are presented as more evolutionarily evolved than the human race because their species has existed for much longer and, as in Darwin's theory, stronger species ultimately end up destroying weaker species.

6 That it is repressive, exploitative and responsible for the genocide of the Tasmanians.

7 That it is physically, morally and psychologically destructive.

8 Much of the world still suffers from famine, warfare and the fear of invasion.

Plot and structure (p. 41)

1 1897.

2 Woking was where he lived and it was also close to London, the heart of the British Empire.

3 Early in the twentieth century.

4 Six years after the invasion.

5 One month.

6 They are taking advantage of the opposition when Mars and the Earth are only 35 million miles apart.

7 Because their own planet is dying.

8 Heat-Ray, tripods, Black Smoke and a flying-machine (although we never see this in action)

9 They have no resistance to Earth's bacteria.

Characterisation (p. 51)

1   A character's actions; a character's dialogue and what other people say about that character; a character's thoughts; the narrator's observations about a character; other characters' comments about themselves and each other; the author's use of language, e.g. imagery and symbolism.

2   The author and his younger brother.

3   To show the hypocrisy of organised religion and as a device for developing the subplot.

4   The artilleryman, because he changes from being an experienced soldier full of sound practical advice to an 'undisciplined dreamer'.

5   The curate, because Wells characterises him with so many disagreeable aspects to his personality such as greediness and childishness.

6   Empire and industrialisation.

Themes (p. 57)

1   Humanity, the Apocalypse, imperialism, war, society and evolution.

2   The human race is capable of great heroism but blighted by the fact that the strong too often prey on the weak.

3   That it is brutal and exploitative.

4   Because the meaningless drudgery that he has the artilleryman describe reflects Wells's two years as an apprentice draper.

5   The Martians.

6   Because the narrator is both excited and horrified by it.

7   Because their warlike behaviour is very similar to man's and because their planet is dying.

Language, style and analysis (p. 65)

1   A writer's style comprises the distinctive characteristics of their work that help to make that writer unique.

2   The narrator's younger brother.

3   Thomas Carlyle.

4   To create the illusion that he is writing a factual rather than a fictional account.

5   It is when an author gives information to the reader that he has withheld from his characters.

6   Because of its emphasis on fast-paced external events and lesser focus on realistically attempting to portray the characters' inner worlds of thought and feeling.

7   The illusion of 'realism', the consequent creation of excitement and a degree of tongue-in-cheek humour.

Tackling the exams (p. 73)

1   No, as it is a 'closed book' examination.

2   In order to make sure that you fully understand the question.

3   In order to ensure that your answer is relevant and fully focused.

4   In order to ensure that you give equal time to all parts of the question.

5   Only if you are entered for OCR.

6   Check your work for obvious SPaG errors and make sure that it makes good sense.

Assessment Objectives and skills (p. 78)

1   Your overall grasp of what the text is about; your ability to express an interpretation of it within the context of the question; your ability to support and develop that interpretation with appropriate textual reference.

2   Your ability to analyse the language, form and structure used by a writer to create meanings and effects, using relevant subject terminology where appropriate.

3   Your ability to show an understanding of the relationships between texts and the contexts in which they were written.

4   The effectiveness and sophistication of your vocabulary and sentence structures and the accuracy of your spelling, punctuation and grammar.

5   AO1 and AO2.

6   Simply retelling the story; quoting long passages; identifying techniques used by an author without explaining what the possible intended effects of these techniques are on the reader; giving unsubstantiated opinions — opinions not backed up by evidence; writing about the characters as if they are real people.

STUDY REVISE AND

for GCSE